"*How to Argue Like Jesus* will help communications professors to teach angelically. Carter and Coleman Christianize Aristotle and add heavenly heuristics that show how Jesus used story and imagery, and how we can go and do likewise."

—MARVIN OLASKY, Provost, The King's College,
New York City; Editor-in-Chief, *World* magazine

"This engaging and edifying study by two gifted Christian writers shows that Jesus understood better than all the others both who he was talking to and what they needed to hear. It turns out that the right kind of straight talk really can confound the smooth experts, and being rhetorically effective doesn't have to be at the expense of your good name. This is a genuine self-help book."

—PETER LAWLER, Dana Professor of Government,
Berry College; author, *Homeless and at Home in America*

"Anti-intellectualism plagues the modern church, but the best response is not a false intellectualism. *How to Argue like Jesus* falls into neither trap. It effectively teaches logic and critical thinking in the context of a well-lived life. This is what the church needs."

—JOHN MARK REYNOLDS, Founder and Director,
Torrey Honors Institute

HOW TO ARGUE LIKE JESUS

HOW TO ARGUE LIKE JESUS

LEARNING PERSUASION FROM HISTORY'S GREATEST COMMUNICATOR

JOE CARTER
JOHN COLEMAN

CROSSWAY
WHEATON, ILLINOIS

How to Argue like Jesus

Published by Crossway
1300 Crescent Street
Wheaton, Illinois 60187

Cover design: Chris Tobias

First printing, 2009

Printed in the United States of America

All emphases in Scripture quotations have been added by the authors.

ISBN-13: 978-1-4335-0271-2
ISBN-10: 1-4335-0271-2
PDF ISBN: 978-1-4335-0559-1
Mobipocket ISBN: 978-1-4335-0560-7
ePub ISBN: 978-1-4335-1861-4

Library of Congress Cataloging-in-Publication Data

Carter, Joe, 1969–
How to argue like Jesus : learning persuasion from history's greatest communicator / Joe Carter and John Coleman.
p. cm.
Includes bibliographical references and index.
ISBN 978-1-4335-0271-2 (tpb)
1. Influence (Psychology)—Religious aspects—Christianity. 2. Persuasion (Psychology). 3. Communication—Religious aspects—Christianity. 4. Jesus Christ—Teaching methods. I. Coleman, John, 1981– . II. Title
BV4597.53.I52C37 2008
232.9'04—dc22 2008014231

Crossway is a publishing ministry of Good News Publishers.

CH 20 19 18 17 16 15 14 13

Joe Carter:
To
Misty and Samantha

John Coleman:
To
Jackie, Shea, John, Chris, and Dustin

CONTENTS

ACKNOWLEDGMENTS

Writing *How to Argue like Jesus* has been a satisfying and truly collaborative effort, and there are dozens of people we must thank for making it a possibility.

We are deeply grateful to Crossway Books for offering two first-time authors a chance to present our ideas and then working tirelessly to make those ideas a reality. In particular, the staff of Crossway Books, including Ted Griffin, Josh Dennis, Amy Stephansen, Justin Taylor, Allan Fisher, and Jill Carter, have spent countless hours encouraging us, editing our work, and pushing to bring this publication to market. Without their diligence, this would not be possible.

We also appreciate the efforts of our friends, peers, colleagues, and mentors who have reviewed portions of the book and offered feedback. Sandy Feit, Peter Lawler, Jackie Coleman, John Mark Reynolds, Jeremy Pierce, Randy Richardson, Chip Hall, Blair Schermerhorn, and Michael Papazian have all supplied comments that made this work inestimably better. We thank them, and we hope they realize the crucial role they played in the final product.

INTRODUCTION
CHRIST THE COMMUNICATOR

His speaking career lasted approximately three years. Born into a Jewish family in an overlooked part of the Roman Empire, Jesus of Nazareth spent most of his thirty-three years working with his hands. We know very little of his early life except that he lived in obscurity. There were exceptional moments: wise men from another empire visited him shortly after his birth; seeking his death, a self-conscious local prefect executed thousands of babies; and at least once he surprised his elders by conversing freely with the religious leaders in the Temple. But apart from these rare moments of distinction, the man who would later launch the world's most popular religion spent 90 percent of his time on earth doing manual labor and living with his humble family, in a humble place, at a time when it was bad to be a Jew and worse to be a Nazarene in a land controlled by Rome.

He was a blue-collar worker with a lower-caste accent, and yet at the age of thirty, he put down his hammer and took to the streets. Speaking to crowds throughout Israel, this carpenter shook the message of traditional Judaism to its core. Where the religious leaders of his day focused on legalism, nationalism, and isolation from the outside world, he preached a message of love, humility, and restoration. Where the textual scholars hid away from the people and exercised a harsh religious code, he preached openness, love, and the need for a salvation that relied not on works but on the grace of God. Where others cast stones, he forgave. Where others passed by the poor, outcast, immoral, and destitute, he fed them, lingered with them, went into their homes, healed them, and spoke with them about their struggles and ideals. Where others saw fishermen, prostitutes, and tax collectors, he saw a group of disciples capable of changing the world.

Jesus never wrote a book, held office, or wielded a sword. He never gained sway with the mighty or influential. He never claimed a political victory. He never took up arms against the governing powers in Rome. Two thousand years after his death, billions of Jews, Muslims, Christians, Hindus, agnostics agree that he never preached a word of hate to gain influence with his followers. He did nothing for which those followers must now be ashamed. He was quiet but firm. He used the spoken word to disseminate a revolutionary message that would eventually spread from a small-town wedding in the deserts of the Middle East to the heights of power in Rome, Western Europe, Africa, and the modern United States.

It's telling that one of Jesus' followers, John, described him quite succinctly as "the Word" (John 1:1, 14). A symbol. A promise. An exhaled message of hope. A piece of communication strong enough to bridge the divide between God and man. The fulfillment of a story thousands of years in the making. It was in part through his revolutionary rhetoric that this humble man rose to prominence as the most influential figure in history.

How did he do it? That's the question we hope to answer, at least partially, with this book. Modern scholars study public figures from Cicero to Hitler with excruciating detail to discover the secrets of their rhetorical success. Laymen reach for books on communication written by professors and CEOs that document the ways in which twenty-first-century businesspeople can succeed in negotiations and motivate their organizations. History buffs read the speeches of Winston Churchill and Abraham Lincoln in search of the proper principles of persuasion. But few people—whether Christians or non-Christians—look back to this man, Jesus of Nazareth, as an example of rhetorical excellence. We read *The Republic* to commemorate the brilliance of Socrates and watch film of Martin Luther King to remember the power of a dream, but we rarely look back to the man whose arguments and speeches in spite of all odds—obscurity, powerlessness, and execution—revolutionized human history.

We hope to illuminate Jesus' method in two ways. First, we'll look at the life and words of Jesus and describe the various ways in which he sought—through the spoken word, his life, and his disciples—to reach others with his message. Second, we'll use the shared artifact of Jesus' life to illuminate some very simple rhetorical lessons that you can use today. A shared artifact is something from our collective past that we can all reference intelligently—a story or thing about which we all know something and through which we can communicate our ideas about a concept or ideal. As the story of Jesus is well known by billions around the world, it presents the perfect opportunity to use his life as a vehicle to explore proper communication techniques.

This is not a scholarly work on rhetoric or communications theory, nor is it a comprehensive account of the message of Jesus or the reasons for its effectiveness in the world. It would be a daunting and nearly impossible task to cover so much ground; and his followers would reject the notion that it was solely the material impact of his communication that spread Christianity (crediting his message in combination with the Holy Spirit, his miracles, and the power of his divinity, at least). But this is an attempt, from a rhetorical perspective, to analyze Jesus' method of communication and the way that method can illuminate our understanding of the subject.

The book is broken into seven chapters. The first three use Aristotle's framework for the three essential components of effective rhetoric—logos, pathos, and ethos—to illuminate the logical, emotional, and personal components of Jesus' message. Aristotle was one of the first great explicators of rhetoric, particularly in his book *On Rhetoric*, and his outline is a remarkably useful way to examine three primary components of Jesus' communication. This is not meant to imply that Jesus was an ardent follower of Aristotle (or a "follower" of any kind); and the authors sincerely believe that we haven't forced the rhetoric of Jesus into the Aristotelian framework. Rather, we believe that through careful study Aristotle identified the same rhetorical truths espoused by Christ—particularly with relation to the concepts of pathos, logos, and ethos—and his explanation remains one of the best ways to illuminate the use of those tools in the rhetoric of others. Many influential Christian philosophers (most notably Thomas Aquinas) have seen parallel truth between some of the philosophies of Greece and the teachings of Christianity; and this is no exception. So rather than dispensing with Aristotle altogether, we'd rather allow the communications of Jesus to further enlighten our understanding of Aristotle's rhetorical frameworks and to solidify the link between those conclusions reached through reason (by means of philosophy) and those reached through revelation (in the person of Jesus).

The fourth chapter, "Narrative and Imagery," seeks to demonstrate Jesus' use of stories and visual imagery to make his words beautiful and memorable. The fifth chapter, "Discipleship," shows how Jesus used the concept of discipleship (or mentorship) in combination with the concept of cellular organizations and small groups to replicate and sustain his message. The sixth chapter, "Heavenly Heuristics," gives a few additional rules of thumb for on-the-fly argumentation, persuasion, and debate. And the final section, "Case Studies," takes these lessons and illuminates them via speeches taken from pop culture and politics.

The authors of this text are believers in the divinity, death, resurrection, and salvific powers of Jesus. These beliefs are reflected in the content of this book. However, we hope this text can be useful to Christians and non-Christians alike; and where possible, we will attempt to focus on the rhetorical techniques of Jesus without moralizing. This is a work for businesspeople, lawyers, stay-at-home moms, students, and anyone else who wants to improve his or her communication. If you would like to be a better communicator, there is no better place to begin than by examining the life, words, and rhetorical strategies of Jesus Christ.

CHAPTER ONE

PATHOS

EMOTIONAL JESUS

On January 28, 1986, a national tragedy supplanted Ronald Reagan's planned State of the Union Address. Early that morning, the *Challenger* space shuttle incinerated in midair over Cape Canaveral, Florida, only minutes after takeoff. As schoolchildren watched from classrooms around the country, seven American astronauts lost their lives, and NASA's push for space exploration came to a standstill. An alarmed populace immediately began to reconsider the cost of an activity that, at times, seemed without purpose.

President Reagan faced the task of mourning seven American heroes and reminding a heartbroken nation of the reasons that in the course of history such sacrifices are sometimes necessary. Unsurprisingly, at a moment of sadness and with little time to speak, the President turned not to lengthy reasoning but to simple emotional appeal. To comfort the nation, President Reagan used pathos.

After listing the names of the astronauts and thanking their families, the President offered these hopeful words:

> We've grown used to wonders in this century. It's hard to dazzle us. But for 25 years the United States space program has been doing just that. We've grown used to the idea of space, and perhaps we forget that we've only just begun. We're still pioneers. They, the members of the *Challenger* crew, were pioneers. . . .
>
> I know it is hard to understand, but sometimes painful things like this happen. It's all part of the process of exploration and discovery. It's all part of taking a chance and expanding man's

> horizons. The future doesn't belong to the fainthearted; it belongs to the brave. The *Challenger* crew was pulling us into the future, and we'll continue to follow them. . . .
>
> We will never forget them, nor the last time we saw them, this morning, as they prepared for their journey and waved goodbye and "slipped the surly bonds of earth" to "touch the face of God."[1]

In a moment of national tragedy, President Reagan appealed not primarily to the intellects of his listeners but to their hearts. He knew that Americans are a nation of immigrants and pioneers. He knew that though Americans might find the long-term rewards of space exploration hard to understand and the tragedy of seven casualties difficult to fathom, they would feel pride that after five hundred years Americans were still exploring, still pushing forward on the frontiers of man, still risking their lives in the pursuit of discovery. He knew that at a time of loss you must assure people that the losses are not in vain. In understanding these simple concepts, President Reagan and his speechwriters crafted one of the most memorable speeches in American history and committed the *Challenger* astronauts to the ages.

The appeal to the heart—pathos—is perhaps the most intuitive of Aristotle's principles. As mentioned in the Introduction, Aristotle literally wrote the book on communication with his treatise *On Rhetoric*, and his categorization of the essential elements of communication (logos, pathos, and ethos) are still useful as we discuss these concepts today. Emotion isn't a learned skill or an acquired capacity but a primal component of human nature. In *On Rhetoric* Aristotle notes, "[There is persuasion] through the hearers when they are led to feel emotion [pathos] by the speech."[2] Three millennia later the power of emotional appeal remains strong.

We can all think of speeches, songs, pictures, or movies that have moved us. We tear up listening to the soulful intonations of Martin Luther King, and our hearts flutter or falter at just the right moments in movies like *It's a Wonderful Life* or *Hotel Rwanda*. Our

[1]Ronald Reagan, "Address to the nation on the Challenger disaster," January 28, 1986; http://www.reaganfoundation.org/reagan/speeches/challenger.asp.
[2]*On Rhetoric*, trans. George A. Kennedy (New York: Oxford University Press, 1991), 38.

emotions are often our catalysts to deeper consideration and action. They give us a fuller picture of the reasons to act on information, encourage us to stand by principle, and add dimension and life to cold fact. As Blaise Pascal phrased it: "The heart has reasons that reason cannot know." Pathos is the essential complement to logos (discussed fully in the next chapter) in human understanding, and just as emotion without reason is hollow and incomplete, logic without emotion is cold and unmoving. Life without feeling is shallow and gray.

Jesus Christ was an exemplary practitioner of the appeal to pathos. Even when his audiences were uneducated or lacked the sophisticated biblical knowledge to fully absorb the power of his religious reasoning, Christ was able to reach their hearts. Through his kindness, his words, and his miracles, Jesus taught his disciples that the way he described was not merely correct but beautiful and comforting and hopeful. Pathos can be abused. But properly used as a complement to reason, emotion adds to the structure of logic the aesthetic of feeling, creating a deeper structure that only our hearts can know.

Of course, knowing that pathos is important and inspiring emotion in those with whom you communicate are two very different things. There are two components to pathos: knowing which appeals are likely to reach listeners and knowing how to implement them effectively. In the following section we discuss both those elements of pathos illuminated by Jesus and the ways in which he communicated them. This is not an exhaustive treatment, and there are surely other ways in which Jesus used pathos to reach audiences, but these are a few key strategies that you can replicate in your daily communication.

IMAGERY AND NARRATIVE STRUCTURE: GIVING EVERY SUBJECT A FACE

In his 1862 work *Fathers and Sons*, Russian novelist Ivan Turgenev wrote, "A picture shows me at a glance what it takes dozens of pages of a book to expound."[3]

[3] See http://www.csuchico.edu/~curbanowicz/syllabi/SYL_113-FA2007.html.

Nothing in rhetoric is as powerful as an image or a narrative. That is why movies have become such dominant media, the visual arts remain so compelling, and storytellers are often the most powerful speakers. People are not moved by abstract moral lessons or logical discussions in the same way they are moved by faces, names, tall tales, and vivid visual imagery. Any discussion of pathos, therefore, must begin with a discussion of imagery and its place in narrative structure.

We will delve deeper into narrative structure in Chapter 4 (which focuses on the overall importance of narrative), but it is useful here to briefly introduce the concepts of narrative and imagery as they relate to pathos before fully exploring them later in the book.

The *American Heritage Dictionary* defines narrative as "a narrated account; a story." The same source defines imagery as "the formation of mental images, figures, or likenesses of things, or of such images collectively." The ancient Greeks even had a term, *enargia*, to refer to "vivid . . . description"[4] that could be inherently moving when depicting things graphic in nature. Intuitively you realize that compelling, graphic accounts of people, places, and things can be stirring, which is why Christ often used visual imagery, particularly within the context of narrative, to create an emotional response in his hearers.

One of Christ's most inspiring uses of narrative and imagery is the Parable of the Good Samaritan, found in Luke 10:30–37.

> Jesus replied, "A man was going down from Jerusalem to Jericho, and he fell among robbers, who stripped him and beat him and departed, leaving him half dead. Now by chance a priest was going down that road, and when he saw him he passed by on the other side. So likewise a Levite, when he came to the place and saw him, passed by on the other side.
>
> "But a Samaritan, as he journeyed, came to where he was, and when he saw him, he had compassion. He went to him and bound up his wounds, pouring on oil and wine. Then he set him on his own animal and brought him to an inn and took care of him. And the next day he took out two denarii and gave them to the innkeeper, saying, 'Take care of him, and whatever more you

[4]See http://rhetoric.byu.edu/figures/E/energia.htm.

> spend, I will repay you when I come back.' Which of these three, do you think, proved to be a neighbor to the man who fell among the robbers?" He said, "The one who showed him mercy."
>
> And Jesus said to him, "You go, and do likewise."

Consider the context of the original audience. The people of the region lived under a series of complex religious and secular laws. The Jewish religious leaders taught the people the truth of their sin nature, but not the hopefulness of God's love. They were often derided by the Pharisees and Sadducees and in many ways must have felt beaten up and abandoned. In other words, *they must have felt a lot like the abandoned man in Jesus' parable*. This is an important point to consider. Jesus was showing that he was on the side of these people, that he had sympathy and love for them. He even specifically called out the fact that a priest (a religious authority) and a Levite (a ruling elite) behaved inhumanely, but a Samaritan (an outcast! a pariah!) made the right choices and gained God's favor.

In this brief story Jesus accomplished several purposes. He showed empathy for his audience, painting their pain in the kind of stunning detail ("stripped him and beat him and departed, leaving him half dead"; "bound up his wounds, pouring on oil and wine") that was sure to make them sit up and pay attention. He also criticized the cold and unfeeling way in which many religious leaders of the time behaved. And in the subtext he showed one group that had suffered hypocrisy (the common people of the region who suffered under pharisaical rule) their own hypocrisy in condemning an even less fortunate group of people (the Samaritans).

In context, Jesus was relating a powerful story that resonated emotionally with the Pharisee who asked the question, with the crowd of diverse people who overheard them, and with the millions of readers who would eventually encounter the parable through Scripture. In an effort to teach people how to be good neighbors—to treat one another properly—Jesus didn't lay out a complex series of rules as the Pharisees were prone to do. Instead he painted a picture of proper behavior that would allow his audience to make commonsense judgments about neighborliness when they encountered their neighbors in the future and would motivate them to remember and follow his maxims.

Of course he often did this with even simpler statements. "Do not throw your pearls before pigs" (Matthew 7:6) is a far more emotionally compelling admonition than "Do not continue to argue with those who refuse to listen." "Why do you see the speck that is in your brother's eye, but do not notice the log that is in your own eye?" (Matthew 7:3) is more jarring than "Why don't you think through the things you have to fix before you spend time thinking about the things your friends have to fix?" Jesus fully understood the importance of imagery to generate pathos and how the use of vivid imagery can enliven communication. Imagery makes a story or word picture more compelling and in doing so excites in us an element of pathos that drab, gray storytelling cannot.

Next time you are giving a speech or writing a paper, begin with a narrative attention-getter—an image that captures the audience's imagination and hearts. Tell someone's story, or paint a picture using metaphor and simile. This can be factual—like using a heart-breaking or hopeful news account from the community—or it can be a fabricated image designed to present a familiar topic in a new way. For example, Aleksandr Solzhenitsyn began his 1970 Nobel Prize lecture[5] with the words:

> Just as that puzzled savage who has picked up—a strange cast-up from the ocean?—something unearthed from the sands?—or an obscure object fallen down from the sky?—intricate in curves, it gleams first dully and then with a bright thrust of light. Just as he turns it this way and that, turns it over, trying to discover what to do with it, trying to discover some mundane function within his own grasp, never dreaming of its higher function.
>
> So also we, holding Art in our hands . . .

Do those words stir something within you that a mere explanation could not? Do all of the extra details ("intricate in curves, it gleams first dully and then with a bright thrust of light") bring the subject to light?

[5] Aleksandr Solzhenitsyn, "Nobel Lecture in Literature 1970," December 10, 1970; http://nobelprize.org/nobel_prizes/literature/laureates/1970/solzhenitsyn-lecture.html.

Again, we will discuss narrative and imagery further in Chapter 4, but for those reading the book piece by piece, it is such an essential component of pathos that it bears repeating.

SHARED VALUES: RELYING ON COMMON BELIEFS

A second method for stirring the hearts of your audience is to utilize shared or common values. As human beings, some concepts inherently move us, and some ethical imperatives compel us to action. At the 1996 State of the World Forum convened by former Soviet President Mikhail Gorbachev, participants from around the world were asked to name five values that mattered most in their daily lives. Truth, compassion, responsibility, freedom, and reverence for life were the values that the diverse group agreed were universal. Indeed, these are intuitively accepted. We all want to be free and happy. We want strong families, good lives, responsible children, and honest and compassionate friends. Because they are universal, you can use these shared values and the words that communicate them both to impact your listeners' emotions and to connect those existing values to new concepts.

Jesus does this brilliantly throughout the four Gospels. While he introduced dozens of radical new concepts, he always did so utilizing the language of the values shared by the Jewish people—love, hope, faith, truth, righteousness, honesty, forgiveness. He often used these established concepts to illuminate new ones that subsequently became shared values (for example, humility, self-sacrifice) and to deepen people's understanding of the values they already shared, extending the application of those values to new arenas.

You can see this in Jesus' statement, "Greater love has no one than this, that someone lay down his life for his friends" (John 15:13), in which Christ uses the shared values of love and friendship to deepen our understanding of the concept of self-sacrifice (which has itself become a shared value because of this and other associations). You can also see it in his Sermon on the Mount. After speaking of the Beatitudes, Jesus reviews a number of concepts including murder, adultery, divorce, and the law—starting with a shared value and using language to deepen his audience's understanding of those values in an emotionally impactful way. Speaking of love, Jesus says:

> "You have heard that it was said, 'An eye for an eye and a tooth for a tooth.' But I say to you, Do not resist the one who is evil. But if anyone slaps you on the right cheek, turn to him the other also. And if anyone would sue you and take your tunic, let him have your cloak as well. And if anyone forces you to go one mile, go with him two miles. Give to the one who begs from you, and do not refuse the one who would borrow from you.
>
> "You have heard that it was said, 'You shall love your neighbor and hate your enemy.' But I say to you, Love your enemies and pray for those who persecute you, so that you may be sons of your Father who is in heaven. For he makes his sun rise on the evil and on the good, and sends rain on the just and on the unjust. For if you love those who love you, what reward do you have? Do not even the tax collectors do the same? And if you greet only your brothers, what more are you doing than others? Do not even the Gentiles do the same? You therefore must be perfect, as your heavenly Father is perfect." (Matthew 5:38–48)

Jesus' audience valued love, but they did so imperfectly—loving only their family and friends. Jesus used the shared value of love, illuminated by the shared values of righteousness and respect for God, to illuminate a stirring new application of love—love for one's enemies.

One of the best modern examples of this is dialogue from the movie *A Few Good Men*. The entire film is an argument for embracing the shared values of honor, freedom, and courage. In the film, a Marine colonel played by Jack Nicholson orders the beating of a young Marine in order to teach the private a lesson about honor and respect for hierarchy. The beating leads to the young man's death and to the court-martial that forms the plot of the story.

On the opposite side, the prosecuting attorney (Tom Cruise) learns that real honor and courage would have involved protecting, rather than abusing, the young Marine. In the pivotal scene between Cruise and Nicholson, the colonel uses an emotional appeal to connect to our shared values:

> Nicholson: You want answers?
> Cruise: I think I'm entitled to them.
> Nicholson: You want answers?!
> Cruise: I want the truth.
> Nicholson (loudly): You can't handle the truth! . . . Son, we live in a world that has walls. And those walls have to be guarded by men with guns. Who's gonna do it? You? You, Lt. Weinberg? I have a greater responsibility than you can possibly fathom. You weep for Santiago and you curse the marines. You have that luxury. You have the luxury of not knowing what I know: That Santiago's death, while tragic, probably saved lives. And my existence, while grotesque and incomprehensible to you, saves lives.
>
> You don't want the truth. Because deep down, in places you don't talk about at parties, you want me on that wall. You [need] me there. We use words like honor, code, loyalty . . . we use these words as the backbone to a life spent defending something. You use 'em as a punchline.
>
> I have neither the time nor the inclination to explain myself to a man who rises and sleeps under the blanket of the very freedom I provide, then questions the manner in which I provide it. I'd prefer you just said thank you and went on your way. Otherwise, I suggest you pick up a weapon and stand a post. Either way, I don't give a [expletive deleted] what you think you're entitled to.[6]

Though Nicholson is ultimately revealed to have betrayed our shared values, his speech is emotionally charged precisely because it contains so many words that resonate with us: truth, responsibility, saving lives, honor, code, loyalty, freedom. Interestingly, the fact that Nicholson's effectiveness was used to harm rather than help also demonstrates how necessary it is to handle pathos with care. Great works are accomplished when human beings are emotionally impacted by rhetoric. But those works can be bad as easily as good, and the rhetor is wholly responsible for assuring that pathos is used to better human existence rather than to harm it.

By using shared values and the words that represent them in your own speech and writing, you will impact hearts and create an emotionally charged response. Shared values make your job easier.

---

[6]Adapted from script found at http://sfy.ru/sfy.html?script=few_good_men. Sorkin, Aaron. Revised third draft, July 15, 1991.

If you can convince members of an audience that a new concept is part of their existing shared values, you do not have to go through the process of proving those values in detail.

SHARED ARTIFACTS: EDUCATING WITH THE FAMILIAR

All communities—be they religious, geographic, ethnic, political, or other—have not only a series of shared values but a collection of shared artifacts. These artifacts are pieces of history that give meaning to a community and provide members of that community with a common set of references, heroes and villains, and stories. For instance, in the United States we have the U.S. Constitution and the stories of our heroic founders (George Washington, Thomas Jefferson, Patrick Henry, and others) that provide us with both a common sense of history and purpose and with a common set of concrete examples to illuminate the values that we share as a culture. In the same way, Christians have biblical artifacts (stories and passages from both the Old and New Testaments); Muslims have Quranic artifacts (stories and passages from the Quran); Greeks have the stories of Homer and the dialogues of Socrates. Smaller communities—such as neighborhoods and families—have their own legends, tall tales, and landmarks. Not all of these are based on fact; but regardless of their foundation, in reality they provide their respective societies with means by which to communicate with one another.

Using these shared artifacts is a remarkably effective way to generate pathos.

Jesus often made use of shared artifacts by utilizing his knowledge of Scripture, geography, and Jewish history.

For instance, after seeing Jesus' disciples plucking grain on the Sabbath, the Pharisees said to him, "Look, your disciples are doing what is not lawful to do on the Sabbath" (Matthew 12:2). Jesus responded by reminding them of a similar historical incident recorded in Scripture:

> He said to them, "Have you not read what David did when he was hungry, and those who were with him: how he entered the

> house of God and ate the bread of the Presence, which it was not lawful for him to eat nor for those who were with him, but only for the priests? Or have you not read in the Law how on the Sabbath the priests in the temple profane the Sabbath and are guiltless?" (vv. 3–5)

This is a typical example of how Jesus handled the complaints of the Pharisees. Throughout the Gospels, Jesus is frequently shown quoting from the shared artifact of Scripture in order to establish that his critics misunderstand God's purposes. The fifteenth chapter of Matthew records another occasion when they chastised Jesus' disciples, this time for failing to adhere to ceremonial hand-washing: "Why do your disciples break the tradition of the elders? For they do not wash their hands when they eat" (Matthew 15:2). Jesus responds by saying:

> "And why do you break the commandment of God for the sake of your tradition? For God commanded, 'Honor your father and your mother,' and, 'Whoever reviles father or mother must surely die.' But you say, 'If anyone tells his father or his mother, "What you would have gained from me is given to God," he need not honor his father.' So for the sake of your tradition you have made void the word of God. You hypocrites! Well did Isaiah prophesy of you, when he said:
>
> *"'This people honors me with their lips,*
> *but their heart is far from me;*
> *in vain do they worship me,*
> *teaching as doctrines the commandments of men.'" (vv. 3–9)*

Rather than conceding their point about his disciples' violation of a tradition, Jesus trumps their concerns by appealing to shared artifacts (the commandments given to Moses and the prophecy of Isaiah) that held greater weight and required stricter adherence.

A more modern example can be found in former U.S. President Bill Clinton's speech to Harvard's 2007 graduating class:

> You've already heard most of what you need to hear today, I think. But I want to focus for a minute on the fact that these graduating

> classes since 1968 have invited a few non-comedians. First was Martin Luther King, who was killed in April before. I remember that very well because it was my senior year at Georgetown. He was killed in April, before he could come and give the speech. And Coretta came and gave the speech for him here. And you've had Mother Teresa and you've had Bono. What do they all have in common? They are symbols of our common humanity and a rebuke even to humorists' cynicism. Martin Luther King basically said he lived the way he did because we were all caught in what he called an inescapable web of mutuality. Nelson Mandela, the world's greatest living example of that, I believe, comes from a tribe in South Africa, the Xhosa, who call it ubuntu. In English, I am because you are. That led Mother Teresa from Albania to spend her life with the poorest people on earth in Calcutta. It led Bono from his rock stage to worry about innocent babies dying of AIDS, and poor people with good minds who never got a chance to follow their dreams. This is a really fascinating time to be a college senior. I was looking at all of you, wishing I could start over again and thinking I'd let you be president if you let me be 21.[7]

Clinton carefully used the history of the venue of his speech (Harvard University) and that particular event's former speakers to generate favorable feelings in his audience in order to prime their emotions for accepting the values he would forward in his own address.

When you are addressing an audience, use shared artifacts in a similar way to impact your listeners emotionally and gain their favor. If you are speaking at a new venue, like a college, use the first part of your speech to elaborate on a favorable quality of that institution or one of its founders—establishing both your knowledge of local history (making *you* one of *them*) and perhaps connecting a value you would like to propose to one already accepted in the shared history of that institution.

If you are having an argument with someone (your brother for instance), speak fondly of someone you both love (e.g., your mother). The shared bond of that artifact may be enough to emotionally diffuse the situation and reinforce the bond itself. Always remember

[7]Remarks of former U.S. President Bill Clinton, *Harvard University Gazette Online*, June 6, 2007; http://www.news.harvard.edu/gazette/2007/06.07/99-clinton.html.

that people are emotionally invested in their families, communities, countries, religions, and cultures. Using the shared artifacts of those groups appropriately will allow you warm entrance into the group and access to the shared values it promotes.

ENERGIA: SHOWING EMOTION

On October 12, 1960, Nikita Khrushchev showed just how powerfully displays of emotion can impact an audience. The hotheaded Soviet leader repeatedly interrupted other delegates at the meeting of the United Nations by taking off his shoe, banging it on the table, and shouting insults, once referring to Filipino delegate Lorenzo Sumulong as "a jerk, a stooge and a lackey of imperialism." Khrushchev let his own emotion pour forth in speech in a way that impacted the pathos of his listeners. Unfortunately for him, his inappropriate use of what the Greeks referred to as *energia* made him look like a buffoon.

One of the greatest ways to create pathos in a speech or a performance is to show that you are genuinely emotionally involved in the subject. This does not involve melodrama or faking it. Being over-the-top or insincere in a display of emotion can kill your connection with an audience—as Nikita Khrushchev, presidential candidate Howard Dean, or any number of failed actors could testify. But showing that you genuinely care about the subject matter of your communication can win your hearers over.

Jesus knew how impactful genuine and appropriate shows of emotion can be. He was not afraid to make an occasional show of emotion—the kind that demonstrated his passion, entrenched his connection with the people of his time, and demonstrated, for everyone, his humanity.

An excellent example is Jesus' famous interaction with the money-changers at the temple. John 2:13–17 records:

> The Passover of the Jews was at hand, and Jesus went up to Jerusalem. In the temple he found those who were selling oxen and sheep and pigeons, and the money-changers sitting there. And making a whip of cords, he drove them all out of the temple, with

> the sheep and oxen. And he poured out the coins of the money-changers and overturned their tables. And he told those who sold the pigeons, "Take these things away; do not make my Father's house a house of trade." His disciples remembered that it was written, "Zeal for your house will consume me."

There were some topics about which Jesus was so passionate he would not censor his emotion, and in this passage his anger (demonstrated as in no other incident in the Gospel narratives) served as a powerful, emotional testament to his passion for the subject—one that likely carried more influence than any sermon on the topic could. Elsewhere Jesus wept over the death of Lazarus (John 11:35) and agonized in the Garden of Gethsemane (Matthew 26:36–45). These displays of emotion by Jesus emotionally charged his listeners and future readers, demonstrated a proper display of anger and mourning, and revealed his own humanity.

We are accustomed to the impact of authentic emotional displays. We recall Andre Agassi crying tears of joy and remembrance as the crowds cheered his last tennis match. We feel knots in our stomachs when Rocky Balboa runs up the steps of the Philadelphia Museum of Art in the original *Rocky* film, jumping for joy when he reaches the top. Our hearts go out to the anguished wife at a funeral and to overjoyed youths victorious in a championship game.

There is a flawed belief that shows of emotion are uncouth or improper. This is not true. While you don't want to descend into melodrama and self-parody, emotion is a powerful and legitimate force in rhetoric. You cannot expect others to become excited or angry about a subject unless you yourself are capable of genuinely reflected emotion.

While you should always be conscious of the appropriateness of the context, don't be afraid to let your emotions pour forth. If you are delivering a prepared speech, you should be more controlled than a person thrown into a heated situation. But if you are overjoyed by a topic, smile and laugh. If you are deeply saddened, do not freeze up if a tear appears in the corner of your eye. If you are angry, make sure your anger is justified, and never let yourself go out of control, but let your audience see your passion. One of the greatest tools of pathos is the emotion you feel inside. Give your audience a glimpse of that passion and humanity and you can win their hearts.

FIGURES OF REPETITION

One of the ways in which you can generate pathos in your readers and listeners is by structuring your rhetoric in musical or poetic ways. There is a reason we all feel compelled to act when listening to rhetors like Martin Luther King or reading the work of writers like Czeslaw Milosz. These people endow their rhetoric with emotional impact by using specific rhetorical figures, or ways of structuring their words, that are memorable, easy to understand, beautiful, and consequently more moving.

Primary to these tactics are figures of repetition. In Latin, the general term for the repetition of a word or words in adjacent phrases or clauses is *conduplicatio*. We will examine four forms of *conduplicatio*—*epizeuxis*, *ploce*, *anaphora*, and *mesodiplosis*.[8] These are complicated words that signify simple methods of utilizing repetitive language.

Epizeuxis is a repetition of words with no others in between, for vehemence or emphasis. Even those who have never read the New Testament are usually familiar with a form of *epizeuxis* as expressed in the King James Version: "Verily, verily, I say unto you . . ."

For example, in John 21:18 Jesus uses the repetition of the word "truly" to emphasize the importance of the passage that follows:

> "Truly, truly, I say to you, when you were young, you used to dress yourself and walk wherever you wanted, but when you are old, you will stretch out your hands, and another will dress you and carry you where you do not want to go."

We've all used this figure of repetition when someone has asked, "Are you happy?" and we responded, "Very, very happy!"

A second strategy, *ploce*, is the repetition of a single word for

[8] All rhetorical terms and definitions are derived from Dr. Gideon Burton, "Silva Rhetoricae"; http://rhetoric.byu.edu/.

rhetorical emphasis. This strategy is an effective means of keeping the focus on the main theme. In Matthew 13, the disciples ask Jesus why he speaks in parables. He answers, "To you it has been given to know the secrets of the kingdom of heaven, but to them it has not been given" (v. 11).

The rest of the chapter records Jesus using the phrase "the kingdom of heaven" seven more times (vv. 24, 31, 33, 44, 45, 47, 52). This repetition helps solidify for his listeners the importance and primacy of the concept. Toward the end of the discourse he asks, "Have you understood all these things?" (v. 51). When they answer, "Yes," Jesus repeats the phrase once again, adding a capstone to his lecture: "Therefore every scribe who has been trained for the kingdom of heaven is like a master of a house, who brings out of his treasure what is new and what is old."

Often you will see the use of recurring phrases or unifying themes throughout speeches and pieces of written rhetoric. Highlighting a key phrase or concept again and again in a piece of communication can assure that the concept is memorable and can endow it with greater emotional weight.

Third, *anaphora* is a type of repetition that uses the same word or group of words at the beginning of successive clauses, lines, or sentences. Similar to this is the fourth strategy, *mesodiplosis*, the repetition of the same word or words in the middle of successive sentences. Taken alone, each can be an effective means of emphasizing a key point. But combined, they can form a powerful framing device that amplifies the parallelism.

In the beginning of his Sermon on the Mount (Matthew 5:3–10), Jesus employs anaphora and mesodiplosis in one of the most beautiful and poetic uses of language ever recorded:

> **Blessed are the** poor in spirit, **for theirs is** the kingdom of heaven.
> **Blessed are those** who mourn, **for they shall** be comforted.
> **Blessed are the** meek, **for they shall** inherit the earth.
> **Blessed are those** who hunger and thirst for righteousness, **for they shall** be satisfied.
> **Blessed are the** merciful, **for they shall** receive mercy.
> **Blessed are the** pure in heart, **for they shall** see God.

Blessed are the peacemakers, **for they shall** be called sons of God.

Blessed are those who are persecuted for righteousness' sake, **for theirs is** the kingdom of heaven.

Our familiarity with this passage can cause us to miss its rhetorical brilliance, particularly in how Jesus is able to draw in the audience. Notice that at the start of the sermon—when his listeners are settling in for his presentation—Jesus starts with a phrase ("Blessed are the") that is non-specific and is not addressed to anyone in particular. Jesus interweaves two uses of anaphora that differ only in the last word in the phrase ("the"/ "those"):

Blessed are the (1)
Blessed are those (2)
Blessed are the (1)
Blessed are those (2)
Blessed are the (1)
Blessed are the (1)
Blessed are the (1)
Blessed are those (2)

Although the change is subtle, it creates a rhythmic pattern: 1, 2, 1, 2, 1, 1, 1, 2.[9]

Now that he has captured the attention of the audience with his musical cadence, Jesus incorporates another subtle shift. Verse 11 begins with a pattern that is similar to the previous ten verses ("Blessed are") but makes a subtle shift from "are the/are those" to "are you." He then uses this new variation to transition into another use of *anaphora* before switching to the *ploce* (repetition of a single word) form:

"**Blessed are you** when others revile **you** and persecute **you** and utter all kinds of evil against **you** falsely on my account."

[9]In the Greek New Testament, this subtle alteration is different but is perhaps even more pronounced. The lines we render in English as "Blessed are those" appear in Greek as the adjective "blessed" followed by a plural definite article and a Greek participle; the phrases we render as "Blessed are the" employ the adjective "blessed" followed by a plural definite article and an adjective.

Having transitioned from "Blessed are the" to "Blessed are you," the term "you" is repeated three times before reversing the pattern from "are you" to "you are" for the beginning of verses 13 ("You are the salt of the earth") and 14 ("You are the light of the world"). Even before his hearers realize what has happened, Jesus has drawn them in and made the sermon about them.

This focus on the self ("Blessed are you . . . you . . . you . . . you . . . your . . . you are . . . you are") appears to continue into verse 16, where the term "your" appears three more times. But once again a subtle but dramatic change occurs. The verse ends by shifting the pattern from the second person plural (you), which puts the emphasis on the listener, to putting the focus and the emphasis on God.

> "In the same way, let your light shine before others, so that they may see your good works and give glory to your Father who is in heaven." (Matthew 5:16)

So how can you use figures of repetition in your rhetoric? In certain, emotionally charged genres of communication, such as a political speech, the answer is obvious. Figures of repetition can make your rhetoric beautiful and allow you to hammer home key thoughts, messages, or phrases with power and emphasis. For instance, when Rev. Martin Luther King Jr. delivered speeches, he almost always used figures of repetition—most famously in his "I Have a Dream" speech.[10] King said:

> I say to you today, my friends, so even though we face the difficulties of today and tomorrow, I still have a dream. It is a dream deeply rooted in the American dream.
>
> I have a dream that one day this nation will rise up and live out the true meaning of its creed: "We hold these truths to be self-evident: that all men are created equal."
>
> I have a dream that one day on the red hills of Georgia, the sons of former slaves and the sons of former slave owners will be able to sit down together at the table of brotherhood.

[10]Martin Luther King Jr., "I Have a Dream," address delivered at the March on Washington for Jobs and Freedom, August 28, 1963; http://www.stanford.edu/group/King/publications/speeches/address_at_march_on_washington.pdf.

> I have a dream that one day even the state of Mississippi, a state sweltering with the heat of injustice, sweltering with the heat of oppression, will be transformed into an oasis of freedom and justice.
>
> I have a dream that my four little children will one day live in a nation where they will not be judged by the color of their skin but by the content of their character.
>
> I have a dream today.

What impacts you the most about King's rhetoric? Almost any listener leaves the speech not only emotionally impacted but with a fuller understanding of King's central focus: aspiration, hope, love—the ethereal substance of dreams. And his use of repetition in that speech left future generations with a similar freedom to dream. This style of speech has been immensely popular in the Christian religious community and can be incredibly effective in sermons and political communications.

In some rhetorical settings (such as in office communications or within a school) it may be harder to conceive of the proper use of repetition, but a measured use of these tools can be similarly effective. If your business has a vision statement or your latest project has a specific, concise aspiration, use figures of repetition to weave that concept throughout your communication so that everyone who receives that communication is fully aware of your focus. Use repeated words to emphasize the seriousness of a given topic (though you should exercise caution—it is easy to overdo it). Also, rather than thinking of communication as dry or dead, think of ways to use the concepts of repetition mentioned above to bring your rhetoric to life.

FIGURES OF PARALLELISM

Another key group of rhetorical strategies are figures of parallelism. During an address to the Roman senate describing his recent victory over an enemy, Julius Caesar showed how the use of parallelism can turn a military victory into memorable rhetoric. To summarize his exploits during the Battle of Zela, Caesar only needed three words: "*Veni, vidi, vici*" ("I came, I saw, I conquered"). What makes the boast memorable is not the action itself (every winning general comes to the battle, sees the enemy, and conquers them) but the terse parallel structure, using the same pattern of words to show that two or more ideas have the same level of importance.

In their book *The Elements of Style*, William Strunk and E. B. White explain that the principle of parallel construction requires that "expressions of similar content and function should be outwardly similar. The likeness of form enables the reader to recognize more readily the likeness of content and function. Familiar instances from the Bible are the Ten Commandments, the Beatitudes, and the petitions of the Lord's Prayer."[11]

Indeed, as Strunk notes, parallelism is one of the most common forms used in the Bible. Psalms and Proverbs provide the most obvious examples, but many examples are found in the Gospels as well.

Synonymous parallelism, one of the most frequent Hebraic poetic structures, is the rhetorical use of synonyms or near synonyms to refer to the same entity or action. The second line or phrase repeats the first, using different words. The last verse of Matthew 11:28–30 provides an example (the parallel clauses are marked A and B):

> "Come to me, all who labor and are heavy laden, and I will give you rest. Take my yoke upon you, and learn from me, for I am gentle and lowly in heart, and you will find rest for your souls. For my yoke is easy (A), and my burden is light (B)."

The opposite of synonymous parallelism is antithetical parallelism, a form in which the repeated terms are opposite in meaning. Luke 6:25 provides two examples:

> Woe to you who are full now (A), for you shall be hungry (B). Woe to you who laugh now (A), for you shall mourn and weep (B).

Chiastic parallelism (or *chiasmus*) is a figure of speech in which the order of the terms in the first of two parallel clauses is reversed

[11]William Strunk, *The Elements of Style* (1918); http://www.bartleby.com/141/strunk5.html.

in the second. If you assign the letters A and B to the first appearance of the key words or phrases and A' and B' to their subsequent appearance, they follow what is commonly referred to as an A-B-B-A pattern. Although this form is more common to Hebrew poetry, there are a few instances, such as in Matthew 3:12, in which Jesus uses *chiasmus*:

> "His winnowing fork is in his hand, and he will clear his threshing floor and gather (A) his wheat (B) into the barn, but the chaff (B) he will burn (A) with unquenchable fire."

The first and fourth lines use different words to describe actions ("gather/burn") that are done to the "wheat/chaff."

Another slightly more complex pattern, ABCCBA, is found in Matthew 13:15. In this example, the vocabulary remains the same:[12]

A "'For this people's heart has grown dull,
B and with their ears they can barely hear,
C and their eyes they have closed,
C' lest they should see with their eyes
B' and hear with their ears
A' and understand with their heart
and turn, and I would heal them.'"

Jesus' use of the chiasmic structure sets up the emotional resonance for the powerful last line.

Chiastic parallelism is particularly useful for oral presentations since the pattern can aid in remembering the material. Many of the stories in Genesis, for example, take this form:

A Chiasm of Concepts (Genesis 11:1–9)

A Human unity (1–2)
B Man speaks and acts (3–4)
C God comes down to see (5)
B' God speaks and acts (6–7)
A' Human dispersion (8–9)

[12]Isaac M. Kikawada and Arthur Quinn, *Before Abraham Was: The Unity of Genesis 1–11* (Ft. Collins, CO: Ignatius Press, 1989), 73.

A Chiasm in the Hebrew Word Order (Genesis 6:8–9)

A Noah
B found favor
C in the eyes of the Lord
D These are the generations of Noah
E Noah was a righteous man
E' perfect he was
D' in his generations
C' with God
B' walked
A' Noah

A Chiasm in the Story of Noah and the Flood (Genesis 6.10–9.19)[13]

A Noah (10a)
B Shem, Ham, and Japheth (10b)
C Ark to be built (14–16)
D Flood announced (17)
E Covenant with Noah (18–20)
F Food in the ark (21)
G Command to enter the ark (7.1–3)
H 7 days waiting for flood (4–5)
I 7 days waiting for flood (7–10)
J Entry to ark (11–15)
K Yahweh shuts Noah in (16)
L 40 days flood (17a)
M Waters increase (17b–18)
N Mountains covered (18–20)
O 150 days waters prevail (21–24)
P GOD REMEMBERS NOAH (8.1)
O' 150 days waters abate (3)
N' Mountain tops become visible (4–5)
M' Waters abate (6)
L' 40 days (end of) (6a)
K' Noah opens window of ark (6b)
J' Raven and dove leave ark (7–9)
I' 7 days waiting for waters to subside (10–11)
H' 7 days waiting for waters to subside (12–13)
G' Command to leave the ark (15–17)
F' Food outside the ark (9.1–4)
E' Covenant with all flesh (8–10)
D' No flood in future (11–17)
C' Ark (18a)
B' Shem, Ham, Japheth (18b)
A' Noah (19)

---

[13]Ibid., 96.

Parallel structures, however, are rarely as intricate and elaborate as chiastic parallelism. Typically they take a form similar to isocolon, a series of similarly structured elements that have the same length and are combined into a series of three parallel elements of the same length, a form known as tricolon. Matthew 7:7–8 provides an example of two tricolons combined to form one thought:

> "Ask, and it will be given to you; seek, and you will find; knock, and it will be opened to you. For everyone who asks receives, and the one who seeks finds, and to the one who knocks it will be opened."

We are all accustomed to uses of parallelism in poetry, theater, and famous historical speeches. Parallelism is, in fact, combined with repetition in the Martin Luther King quotation in the previous section. Unfortunately, we often get caught in the trap of thinking only great writers and speakers can employ these tools. On the contrary, every rhetor can improve himself or herself by thinking about ways in which he or she can use these more advanced figures, forms, and structures to improve his or her own communications.

In school, highlight similar points with parallel structure, and use a tricolon to point out a series of three points in an aesthetically pleasing, emotionally impactful way. At work, make vision statements and strategies more compelling by structuring them in parallel or repetitive ways that make them more memorable and powerful. In your sermons, take the time to review the messages you write, and see if there are ways to enliven particular passages using parallel structures that will make it easier for your congregation to absorb and follow your message.

You don't have to master complex chiasms to use figures of parallelism (though it's a powerful statement of the Bible's literary greatness that it effectively employs those structures). Start with the basics, and build the aesthetics of your communication.

QUESTIONS: ASKING FOR ANSWERS TO OPEN THEIR MINDS

Finally, one of the most effective ways to generate pathos and grab an audience's attention is to ask questions. By asking your listeners something rather than preaching to them or giving them answers, you let them come to their own conclusions, which often forces them to be more emotionally and intellectually attached to those conclusions.

In the chapter on logos, we talk about how a particular logical tool called the enthymeme allows an audience to complete a logical chain, making the audience more intellectually involved in the logic itself. Asking questions generates the same rhetorical effect. This is, at least partially, what the Greeks referred to as *epiplexis* (asking questions in order to chide, to express grief, or to inveigh), though it also extends to questions that cause an audience to draw positive or joyful conclusions.

On a number of occasions Jesus used the power of a question to impact his listeners' emotions.

In one famous example, the disciples are discussing what people think of Jesus, and he forces them to personalize the issue with a question. Matthew 16:13–15 records:

> Now when Jesus came into the district of Caesarea Philippi, he asked his disciples, "Who do people say that the Son of Man is?" And they said, "Some say John the Baptist, others say Elijah, and others Jeremiah or one of the prophets." He said to them, "But who do you say that I am?"

By asking a question, Jesus turns an intellectual discussion (what others have to say about Jesus) into a personal, emotional decision (what do I think?). In Luke 7:24–26, Jesus forces people to confront their fascination with John the Baptist and the reason for that fascination by asking emotional questions. Luke writes:

> When John's messengers had gone, Jesus began to speak to the crowds concerning John: "What did you go out into the wilderness to see? A reed shaken by the wind? What then did you go

> out to see? A man dressed in soft clothing? Behold, those who are dressed in splendid clothing and live in luxury are in kings' courts. What then did you go out to see? A prophet? Yes, I tell you, and more than a prophet."

Throughout the New Testament, Jesus uses questions to force people to personalize answers, to come to obvious conclusions, and to take emotional and intellectual ownership of those conclusions.

Where can you incorporate this into your communications? At McKinsey & Company, consultants often use questions in their presentations (usually in the form of callouts—short sentences in highlighted boxes that refer to a series of graphs, data, or conclusions) to force teams to think hard about presented information and draw their own conclusions; and doing so can be far more intellectually and emotionally powerful than presenting the supposed answers outright. In speech, good orators will often pose compelling questions at the beginning of their presentations to get the audience thinking about a subject, switching them from content absorption mode to content consideration mode. These orators make listeners participants in the speech, not observers. Similarly, good parents often phrase their parental instructions in the form of questions: "If everyone else was jumping off a bridge, would you?"

Questions, well placed and used sparingly, can be powerful, emotional punctuations to a piece of communication that force your audiences to turn on their brains and really take ownership of the content at hand.

CONCEPT REVIEW

Pathos: Emotional appeal.

Narrative: A narrated account; a story.

Imagery: The formation of mental images, figures, or likenesses of things or of such images collectively.

Shared values: Values that many people hold in common.

Shared artifacts: Past events, stories, or pieces of communication (e.g., the Bible, the works of Shakespeare, the life of Jesus Christ) with which the majority of an audience is familiar.

Energia: A genuine and appropriate show of emotion.

Figures of repetition: Uses of the repetition of words, phrases, or structures to generate pathos.

Figures of parallelism: Using the same pattern of words to show that two or more ideas have the same level of importance.

QUESTIONS FOR FURTHER CONSIDERATION

1. Why is it important that Jesus used pathos in his communication? What does Jesus' use of pathos say about the importance of human emotion?
2. How could the church benefit from a deeper recognition of the importance of pathos in human communication?
3. In what ways are Christians properly applying pathos to public life? In what ways are Christians poorly applying those principles?
4. Where do you most often encounter pathos?
5. Identify a recent piece of your own communication—a memo, sermon, PowerPoint, essay, or thank-you card. Reread it. Can you spot additional places in which you might have employed pathos?
6. Think of your favorite movie scene. What elements of that scene caused it to be so powerful?

CHAPTER TWO

LOGOS

JESUS THE LOGICIAN

A SHORT HISTORY OF LOGIC: REASONS FOR REASON

Whenever we communicate, we attempt to support our communication with reason. At work, you use financial projections, customer surveys, and focus groups to make sure you've grounded your business presentations in fact. When you vote, you look to political leaders who can give reasons for their positions so that you can evaluate those reasons and choose a candidate accordingly. In your personal life, you make logical excuses to wives, husbands, parents, and girlfriends to explain loaded dishwashers, late dinners, and lingering trash cans. You employ the tools of logic every day; you probably just don't look at these tools in a structured way. You instinctively know when you've heard a good or bad argument, but often you don't know why.

Nearly three thousand years ago Aristotle formulated a method for logical communication. Along with a few Greek contemporaries like Plato and Euclid, Aristotle laid the groundwork for Western logical development and formulated the formal principles for applying logic to rhetoric, cementing *logos* (logic) as one of his three primary rhetorical tenets. Logical reasoning was the basis of Socrates' dialectic and in turn the basis for modern debate. Over time various Western thinkers—William of Ockham, Adam Smith, Immanuel Kant, and others—used this groundwork to build the canon of Western thought. Logic is the central way in which most Western philosophers seek to organize and describe human behavior; it is the bedrock of modern science.

Outside the West, other cultures place a similar importance on logic. In China, the philosopher Mozi founded the Mohist School, creating the basis for a Chinese logic that placed a heavier emphasis on the confinement of logical truths to a specific time and place than did Aristotle. Mozi also emphasized common issues such as valid inference and correct conclusions. In India, Nyaya and Vaisheshika, two of the six schools of Indian thought, deal with logic, employing even more complex decision-making criteria than Aristotle. Islam, partially developed employing Aristotelian systems of thought, made extensive use of logic and reasoning in the construction of its laws and codes.

Almost anywhere you go, the logical consistency of your communication—your appeals to reason—will be essential to your ability to impact listeners.

Communicating a message effectively requires substantial use of logic, and you cannot discern good reasoning from bad without a detailed understanding of the way in which logical connections are built into rhetoric. "Persuasion," said Aristotle, "occurs . . . when we show the truth or apparent truth from whatever is persuasive in each case."[1]

As a communicator eminently concerned with both persuasion and truth (the claim that there is an absolute, a logical consistency to existence), Jesus knew that his listeners expected logical consistency in his arguments. Understanding this basic premise will not only allow us to imitate his example—more effectively utilizing reason in our own communications—but to remember that Jesus' proper place in history is multifaceted. While many modern anti-theists argue for the irrationality of religion, Jesus is an exemplar of reason, rationality, and logic.

What follows is a technique-by-technique evaluation of some of the specific ways Jesus employed logic in his rhetoric, specifically focused on eight techniques: syllogism, enthymeme, *syllogismus*, *a fortiori*, *reductio ad absurdum*, false dilemma, appeal to evidence, and the cumulative case. These techniques are not confined to Christian rhetoric—far from it. They are, instead, widely accepted principles of rhetoric and argumentation that people have used for

[1] Aristotle, *On Rhetoric*, trans. George A. Kennedy (New York: Oxford University Press, 1991), 39.

centuries and that we can see clearly implemented by the person of Jesus Christ.

This is not a complete list of the ways Jesus used logic, nor is it comprehensive of the various logical forms at your disposal; but it does make a critical point. Jesus used facts, and his arguments made sense. If you are going to be an effective communicator, you must do the same.

SYLLOGISM: PUTTING YOUR THOUGHTS INTO LOGICAL CHAINS

A syllogism is a sequence of two statements, called premises, the truth of which implies the truth of a third statement, known as conclusion. The term for deriving a conclusion from something known or assumed is "deduce,"[2] which is why syllogisms are forms of deductive arguments. In a good deductive argument, if the premises are true, then the conclusion must be true. For example:

> All dogs are mammals.
> All mammals are animals.
> Therefore, all dogs are animals.

In this example, if we accept the truth of the first two statements, then we must also accept the truth of the conclusion. Notice there is an underlying pattern to our example. If we substitute the terms (dogs, mammals, and animals) for letters (A, B, C) the pattern becomes more obvious:

> All A are B.
> All B are C.
> Therefore, all A are C.

In the New Testament, Jesus rarely used full syllogisms, relying instead on an even more powerful syllogistic form known as the

[2]Here it is important to note an important distinction in logic—that between deduction and induction. Deductive logic involves moving from a generally accepted principle or truth to a specific conclusion. As an example, if we believe in the general principle of gravity, we believe that any dropped object (like an apple) will fall to the ground. Inductive logic, on the other hand, involves moving from specific observations to a general principle or conclusion. For instance, if I witness enough apples, oranges, and bananas falling to the ground, I may inductively arrive at the general principle of gravity.

enthymeme (discussed in the next section); but the syllogism is the basic foundation of much of Jesus' rhetoric, and a basic understanding of the syllogism is necessary for an understanding of its various forms and of the concept of logic itself.

The finest exemplars of the full syllogism may be the legendary philosopher Socrates and his successors, Plato and Aristotle (the latter coined the term syllogism). In Book I of *The Republic*, Socrates, seeking to prove that all things have "ends" or purposes, says:

> *Socrates:* And the end or use of a horse or of anything would be that which could not be accomplished, or not so well accomplished, by any other thing?
>
> *Thrasymachus:* I do not understand.
>
> *Socrates:* Let me explain: Can you see, except with the eye?
>
> *Thrasymachus:* Certainly not.
>
> *Socrates:* Or hear, except with the ear?
>
> *Thrasymachus:* No.
>
> *Socrates:* These then may be truly said to be the ends of these organs?[3]

Though a bit more difficult to discern (because it is surrounded by supporting text), Socrates is forwarding a simple syllogism.

> 1. The purpose of a thing is that which could not be accomplished by any other thing.
> 2. Seeing could not be accomplished by any thing other than the eye.
> 3. The eye has a purpose.

In practice, syllogisms are often more than three statements—they are simply strings of logical thought known as polysyllogisms or multi-premise syllogisms in which the conclusion of one syllogism serves as the premise for the next; and often this is condensed to a *sorites* (Greek for "heap" or "pile"), which is just a chain of propositions that lead to a conclusion. The concept of polysyllogism

[3]Plato, Book I, *The Republic*; http://www.sacred-texts.com/cla/plato/rep/rep0110.htm.

or *sorites,* therefore, allows you to move beyond simple two- or three-line statements to complex chains of logical thought.

So why is the syllogism important for you?

The syllogism is at the heart of basic logic—the ability to connect facts using reason to draw new conclusions. Understanding this logical form will better help you understand Jesus' use of logic and the ways in which you can make your own arguments make sense. Knowing how to properly use syllogisms will help you influence others, and knowing how to find faults in syllogisms will help you avoid mistakes in logical reasoning when communicating.

For example, one popular fallacious polysyllogism proceeds:

1. God is love.
2. Love is blind.
3. Ray Charles is blind.
4. Ray Charles is God.

Once we reach the conclusion of this argument, we realize that it is silly, but can you spot the biggest mistake? In sentence 2, the statement "love is blind" is meant to imply that all love is blind, but it is taken to imply that all blind things (like Ray Charles) are love. There are other fallacies in the statement, but this is the most obvious and leads to the false conclusion that Ray Charles is God.

When dealing with logic chains, it is always important to question both the validity of each statement or premise (Is love really blind? What does that mean?) and the connections between statements (Is all love blind, or are all blind things love?). Incorrectly constructing a syllogism can cause you to mislead a reader or listener. Accepting an invalid syllogism can lead you to absurd conclusions.

ENTHYMEME: MAKING YOUR LOGIC CHAINS MORE COMPELLING

As mentioned, one rarely finds a syllogism in its pure form, particularly in the rhetoric of Jesus. Instead syllogisms are often found in an abbreviated and more powerful form in which a premise or conclusion is merely implied. For instance, consider this truncated form of our first syllogistic example:

> Dogs are mammals; therefore they are animals.

In this argument, the first premise (All mammals are animals) is implied. This is an example of what logicians call an enthymeme, a way of presenting a deductive argument in which one of the elements is left unstated.

There are three particular forms that an enthymeme can take:

1. Major premise + minor premise: *All mammals are animals, and all dogs are mammals.*
2. Conclusion + major premise: *Dogs are animals because all mammals are animals.*
3. Conclusion + minor premise: *Dogs are animals because dogs are mammals.*

If you analyze the discussions Jesus had with the scribes and Pharisees, you'll recognize that one of his most frequently used rhetorical devices was the enthymeme. Jesus used enthymemes because they are a particularly effective form of argument. In most cases enthymemes identify the conclusion that is to be accepted before proceeding to identify what is to be argued for (the minor premise). As Dallas Willard notes in his essay "Jesus the Logician":

> [Jesus'] use of logic is always enthymemic, as is common to ordinary life and conversation. His points are, with respect to logical explicitness, understated and underdeveloped. The significance of the enthymeme is that it enlists the mind of the hearer or hearers from the inside, in a way that full and explicit statement of argument cannot do. Its rhetorical force is, accordingly, quite different from that of fully explicated argumentation, which tends to distance the hearer from the force of logic by locating it outside of his own mind.[4]

[4]Dallas Willard, "Jesus the Logician," *Christian Scholar's Review* 28.4 (Summer 1999), 605–614; http://www.dwillard.org/articles/artview.asp?artID=39.

Rather than force a particular conclusion upon someone by the sheer weight of logic, Jesus would allow his audience to "connect the dots" and discover the insight on their own. This is another example of Jesus' profound understanding of human nature. People are often resistant to accepting "foreign" ideas but are less hesitant when the conclusion is deduced from their own thought processes. By leaving steps out, he allowed listeners to complete the argument themselves, internalizing it and amplifying its power.

Jesus' purpose is not to score points in a debate or to earn a hollow victory for his position. "Jesus' aim in utilizing logic is not to win battles," says Willard, "but to achieve understanding or insight in his hearers."[5] By having a thorough understanding of logical relations and implementing them in an effective rhetorical form, Jesus' words transformed the world. If our words are to do the same, we would do well to imitate his methods.

Let's start by examining some of the ways that Jesus used enthymemes and syllogistic forms.

Again, the hypothetical syllogism states that if A implies B, and B implies C, then A implies C. This syllogism takes the following form:

> If A then B.
> If B then C.
> Therefore, if A then C.

An example of Jesus' use of the hypothetical syllogism can be found in Matthew 10. As he prepares his disciples to go out and preach "to the lost sheep of the house of Israel" (v. 6), Jesus encourages them by saying, "Whoever receives you receives me, and whoever receives me receives him who sent me" (v. 40).

In this example the hypothetical syllogism takes the form of an enthymeme in which the conclusion is merely implied:

> If A (someone receives you), then B (that person is receiving me).

[5]Ibid.

If B (someone receives me), then C (that person is receiving the one who sent me).

Therefore, if A (someone receives you), then C (that person is receiving the one who sent me).

Although he doesn't state the conclusion explicitly, Jesus is saying that anyone who receives the disciples and the message they are preaching is receiving the Father.

The fifth chapter of John provides several examples of enthymemes used by both Jesus and by the Pharisees. After healing an invalid, Jesus tells the man, "Get up, take up your bed, and walk" (v. 8). When the Pharisees see the man carrying his bed on the Sabbath they say to him, "It is the Sabbath, and it is not lawful for you to take up your bed" (v. 10).

Here the Pharisees use an abbreviated form (combining the conclusion and the minor premise) of the *modus ponens*, a common type of syllogism. The *modus ponens* takes the form of:

If A then B.
A,
Therefore B.

The Pharisees' argument, which includes a conclusion, a minor premise, and an implied major premise, could be outlined as:

If it is the Sabbath, then it is unlawful to do work like carrying a bed.

It is the Sabbath.

Therefore, it is unlawful to do work like carrying a bed.

If the premises are true (it is unlawful to work on the Sabbath, it is necessary to behave in a way that is lawful, it is the Sabbath), then this is a good deductive argument. The Pharisees certainly believe the premises are true, and the healed man doesn't appear to disagree. When they confront Jesus with this argument, however, he answers with his own enthymemic claim that he is equal with God:

"My Father is working until now, and I am working" (v. 17).

His abbreviated argument can be outlined as:

> God the Father is working even though it is the Sabbath.
> I am equal to God the Father.
> Therefore, I am working even though it is the Sabbath.

The Pharisees instantly recognized the "blasphemous" claim that Jesus was making: "This was why the Jews were seeking all the more to kill him, because not only was he breaking the Sabbath, but he was even calling God his own Father, making himself equal with God" (v. 18).

As they were two thousand years ago, enthymemes are powerful statements that arise daily in our conversations. We see enthymemes in our offices, classrooms, homes, and political forums.

As an example, if your business colleague tells you to avoid a particular course of action because it would be unprofitable, he is using an enthymeme. He argues:

1. Your business activity is only valid if it reaps a profit. (unstated premise)
2. It will not reap a profit.
3. It is not a valid activity.

By shortening the statement to, "You shouldn't sell product x because it is unprofitable," he makes the logical chain pithier and more compelling. However, you have the power to counter this argument if either the purpose of the activity is not to reap a profit (and thus the unstated premise of the syllogism is faulty) or if you do not accept the premise that the activity will be unprofitable. Being able to recognize the structure of his argument is essential for showing where it errs.

Whenever you see someone argue using an enthymeme, try to figure out the unstated portion of the logical chain, and, as with the syllogism, test the validity of the premises as Jesus often did with the Pharisees. When you are presenting a logical case to someone, think about using enthymemes rather than full syllogisms (leaving some portions of the argument unstated rather than fully completing them). Doing so may more fully engage your audience, and if they draw the same conclusions, it will give them more ownership of the argument you're putting forth.

SYLLOGISMUS: SHORTENING THE SYLLOGISM TO A SOUND BITE

A further, even more compact form of the syllogism is known as the *syllogismus* (not to be confused with the syllogism). The *syllogismus* is the use of a remark or an image that calls upon the audience to draw an obvious conclusion. This form is similar to an enthymeme, though more compact, and frequently relies on an image. An example of the *syllogismus* can be found in Luke 7:44–46:

> Then turning toward the woman he said to Simon, "Do you see this woman? I entered your house; you gave me no water for my feet, but she has wet my feet with her tears and wiped them with her hair. You gave me no kiss, but from the time I came in she has not ceased to kiss my feet. You did not anoint my head with oil, but she has anointed my feet with ointment."

Jesus provides examples of what the woman has done for him (wet his feet with her tears, wiped them with her hair, kissed them, and anointed them with ointment) in order to create an image of how someone who loves him would act. The conclusion to be drawn, though left unstated, is that the woman loves Jesus more than Simon does.

Syllogismus is compelling both for its logic and for its imagery (which often doubles as an emotional appeal).

When former U.S. President Bill Clinton remarked, "I feel your pain," he was relying on *syllogismus*. Clinton had an unstated premise (that the people in his audience were in pain), and by stating that he felt or understood that pain he expected that audience to both connect with him and to believe he had the necessary understanding and motivation to address the causes and implications of that pain (the obvious conclusion the audience might draw).

The *syllogismus* can be an effective tool, but use it with caution. Due to its use of imagery (and thus emotional appeal) and compact forms of logic, it is more powerful than tools like the full syllogism and more easily abused. Jesus used *syllogismus* to bring his points to life, to give listeners even more information to interpret, and to reach audiences who did not need overt preaching but rather an opportunity to reach their own conclusions with a little careful guidance. When you use *syllogismus*, be careful not to abuse the technique. A few deceptive or abusive statements and your audiences won't be fooled—but they will begin to mistrust you.

A FORTIORI: PLAYING TO YOUR STRENGTHS

Another figure of reasoning that Jesus was particularly fond of using is the *a fortiori* (Latin for "to the stronger," or "even more so") argument. As philosopher Douglas Groothuis explains in his article "Jesus: Philosopher and Apologist," these arguments take the following form:

> 1. The truth of idea A is accepted.
> 2. Support for the truth of idea B (which is relevantly similar to idea A) is even stronger than that of idea A.
> 3. Therefore, if the truth of idea A must be accepted, then so must the truth of idea B be accepted.[6]

We are bound to accept an *a fortiori* claim because of our prior acceptance of a weaker application of the same reasoning or truth. Because the scribes and Pharisees were constantly accusing him of Sabbath-breaking, Jesus was able to effectively employ *a fortiori* arguments against them.

> Jesus answered them, "I did one work [on the Sabbath], and you all marvel at it. Moses gave you circumcision (not that it is from Moses, but from the fathers), and you circumcise a man on the Sabbath. If on the Sabbath a man receives circumcision, so that the law of Moses may not be broken, are you angry with me because on the Sabbath I made a man's whole body well? Do not judge by appearances, but judge with right judgment." (John 7:21–24)

[6]Douglas Groothuis, "Jesus: Philosopher and Apologist," *Christian Research Journal*, Vol. 25, No. 2 (2002); http://www.equip.org/site/c.muI1LaMNJrE/b.2628317/k.B78D/DJ700.htm.

Groothuis succinctly outlines Jesus' argument as follows:

> 1. The Pharisees endorse circumcision, even when it is done on the Sabbath, the day of rest from work. (Circumcision was performed eight days after the birth of a male, which sometimes fell on the seventh day of the week, the Sabbath.) This does not violate the Sabbath laws, because it is an act of goodness.
>
> 2. Healing the whole person is even more important and beneficial than circumcision, which affects only one aspect of the male.
>
> 3. Therefore, if circumcision on the Sabbath is not a violation of the Sabbath, neither is Jesus' healing of a person on the Sabbath.

He adds: "Jesus' concluding comment, 'Stop judging by appearances, and make a right judgment,' was a rebuke to their illogical inconsistency while applying their own moral and religious principles."[7]

A fortiori arguments are exceptionally useful in communication as tools for pointing out the inconsistency of an action, policy, or statement.

In an address to fellow ministers known as "Letter from Birmingham Jail," Martin Luther King used *a fortiori* argument to point out inconsistencies in the way white ministers were dealing with the oppression of African-Americans in the region. Noting that the ministers were more concerned with black demonstrations in the city than with the oppression that led to the demonstrations, King stated:

> You deplore the demonstrations taking place in Birmingham. But your statement, I am sorry to say, fails to express a similar concern for the conditions that brought about the demonstrations. I am sure that none of you would want to rest content with the superficial kind of social analysis that deals merely with effects and does not grapple with underlying causes. It is unfortunate that demonstrations are taking place in Birmingham, but it is even more unfortunate that the city's white power structure left the Negro community with no alternative.[8]

[7]Ibid.

[8]Martin Luther King Jr., "Letter from Birmingham Jail," April 16, 1963; http://www.stanford.edu/group/King/popular_requests/frequentdocs/birmingham.pdf.

This is a powerful and classical argument—the same Jesus often levied against the Pharisees—and it is likely that King, a minister of the gospel, pulled many of his rhetorical tools, including *a fortiori*, from a careful reading of the life of Jesus.

Where can you use *a fortiori*? It is a particularly useful tool when people have misordered priorities. Sometimes churches focus on small points of theological dispute at the expense of major doctrinal issues, and *a fortiori*, properly applied, can help people refocus on the most important issues.

In politics, *a fortiori* can serve the same purpose. In the U.S. one might draw on *a fortiori* to point out that if we have the freedom to say offensive or abrasive things in public (curse words, insults, etc.), the case for the continued freedom of more virtuous speech (like prayer) in public places should be even stronger.

As with other techniques of logos, be careful not to abuse *a fortiori*. People are often sensitive when you criticize them for inconsistency, and sometimes they respond negatively to comparisons aimed at pointing out hypocrisy. When your wife asks you to take out the trash, it is usually a bad time to point out that *Monday Night Football* is more important; and when your parents prevent you from attending a party where there may be questionable behavior, do not respond by pointing out that you are in environments with even more questionable behavior all the time. If you do, you might not like the result!

REDUCTIO AD ABSURDUM: TAKING AN ARGUMENT TO ITS CONCLUSION

Reductio ad absurdum (Latin for "reduction to the absurd") is a type of logical argument where one assumes a claim for the sake of argument, derives an absurd or ridiculous outcome, and then concludes that the original assumption must have been wrong, as it led to an absurd result. This type of argument is frequently used by rhetoricians and philosophers and was used to masterly effect by Jesus.

The twelfth chapter of Matthew provides a prime example. After healing a man who was oppressed by demons, the Pharisees said of Jesus, "It is only by Beelzebul, the prince of demons, that this man casts out demons" (v. 24). Their claim was that Jesus was able to command the demons because he was given authority by the demon-in-chief. To point out the absurdity of their claims, Jesus responded:

> "Every kingdom divided against itself is laid waste, and no city or house divided against itself will stand. And if Satan casts out Satan, he is divided against himself. How then will his kingdom stand?" (vv. 25–26)

Reductio ad absurdum is a good and necessary way to work through the logical implications of a position. Most of Plato's *Republic* is an account of Socrates' attempts to guide listeners to the logical conclusions of their beliefs about justice, democracy, and friendship, among other concepts, through extended bouts of *reductio ad absurdum*. The United States Supreme Court also used this technique when it handed down its ruling in the famous 1954 case *Brown v. Board of Education*. F. A. Hayek used the principle of *reductio ad absurdum* to point out the problems with totalitarianism in his work *The Road to Serfdom*, and it is a favorite tool of classic mathematicians such as Euclid. While *reductio ad absurdum* can lead to long and complex arguments, it is often quite simple and practically useful. Take the following conversation as an example:

> Mother (seeing her child take a rock from the Acropolis): You shouldn't do that!
>
> Child: Why not? It is just one rock!
>
> Mother: Yes, but if everyone took a rock, it would ruin the site!

The mother states that if everyone took the child's actions, an archaeological site would be decimated. As you can see, the use of *reductio ad absurdum* can be remarkably effective, whether in complex judicial arguments or in everyday conversations.

However, it is easy to move from *reductio ad absurdum* to what some people call the slippery slope fallacy.[9] The slippery slope fallacy uses a logic chain similar to that employed in *reductio ad absurdum* that makes unreasonable logical jumps, many of which involve so-called "psychological continuums" that are highly unlikely.

For example, many proponents of harsh penalties for marijuana possession argue that it is a stepping-stone to more extreme behavior like heroin use. That is seemingly why some countries like Saudi Arabia and Singapore impose capital punishment for drug trafficking. Many opponents of harsh marijuana laws argue (rightly or wrongly) that the slippery slope is fallacious and that penalties for marijuana use should be judged on the immediate effects and dangers of that drug rather than on where such use might lead.

FALSE DILEMMA AVOIDANCE: THINKING OUTSIDE THE BOX

Not all logical principles involve the creation of proper arguments—some involve the ability to spot and counter fallacious arguments. One of the most common logical fallacies that Jesus encountered is the false dilemma. The logical fallacy of false dilemma involves a situation in which two alternative points of view are held to be the only options, when in reality there exists one or more other options that have not been considered. Jesus used this form of reasoning when the religious authorities would try to trap him into accepting statements with which he did not agree.

Although Jesus often debated with the scribes and Pharisees, there are only two recorded examples of his speaking with the members of the ruling elite, the Sadducees (though one is recorded in all three of the Synoptic Gospels—Matthew 22:23–34; Mark 12:18–27; Luke 20:27–40). The other occasion is seen in Matthew 16:1–4. The Sadducees were theological and religious conservatives who did not recognize the rest of the Hebrew canon beyond the Torah. In a ploy to trap Jesus, the Sadducees attempted to

[9]In reality, slippery-slope argument can be both valid and invalid, but it is useful here to differentiate between *reductio ad absurdum* and its fallacious counterpart by referring to the fallacy as slippery slope. For a full treatment of slippery slope, a useful resource is Eugene Volokh, "The Mechanisms of the Slippery Slope"; http://www.law.ucla.edu/volokh/slippery.pdf.

show that his prophecy of a future resurrection meant he denied the Torah:

> And Sadducees came to him, who say that there is no resurrection. And they asked him a question, saying, "Teacher, Moses wrote for us that if a man's brother dies and leaves a wife, but leaves no child, the man must take the widow and raise up offspring for his brother. There were seven brothers; the first took a wife, and when he died left no offspring. And the second took her, and died, leaving no offspring. And the third likewise. And the seven left no offspring. Last of all the woman also died. In the resurrection, when they rise again, whose wife will she be? For the seven had her as wife." (Mark 12:18–23)

As philosopher Jeremy Pierce illustrates, the reasoning of the Sadducees takes the following form:

1. If we believe the Torah's teaching on Levirate marriage, then we have to deny the doctrine of the resurrection.
2. The Torah's teaching on Levirate marriage is unquestionable.
3. Therefore, the doctrine of resurrection must be wrong.[10]

Jesus' response shows that the Sadducees were offering a false dilemma. Jesus responded by saying:

> "Is this not the reason you are wrong, because you know neither the Scriptures nor the power of God? For when they rise from the dead, they neither marry nor are given in marriage, but are like angels in heaven." (Mark 12:24–25)

Whereas the Sadducees present two mutually exclusive options—accept the Torah's teaching and deny the resurrection or accept the resurrection but deny the Torah—Jesus offers a third explanation: marriage is an institution that won't exist in the post-resurrection world. This response would have still been rejected by the Sadducees, but it showed that Jesus was neither rejecting the authority of the Torah nor committing a logical fallacy.

[10] Jeremy Pierce, "Jesus' Reasoning in Mark 12:18-27; Matt 22:23-34; Luke 20:27-40," February 1, 2005; http://parablemania.ektopos.com/archives/2005/02/jesus_reasoning_6.html.

Knowing how to spot and avoid false dilemmas is essential for anyone interested in effective argumentation and debate. False dilemmas are common in politics, office interactions, and family and church life. In politics you may hear a statement like "Either we raise taxes or we will have to stop medical care for the elderly" when in reality there may be a number of other ways to sustain that care even in a lower tax environment. At church you may hear someone say, "Either you believe in biblical inerrancy or you are not a Christian" when there are obviously a number of well-meaning Christians who believe certain portions of the Bible to be in error. At home you may hear your daughter complain, "If you don't buy me a car, you don't love me" when in reality there are a number of good alternative explanations for why you might not buy your teenager a new Honda.

Whenever someone presents you with an either/or dilemma, ask yourself, as Jesus did, whether there is an alternative explanation. Many issues in the world are not black and white, either/or. Don't let people trap you into agreeing with one thing when an alternative may exist.

APPEAL TO EVIDENCE: USING FACT-BASED THINKING

One of the most important elements of logos is the appeal to evidence—what management consultants often refer to as "fact-based" thinking. When you make an argument, it is often important that it not only make sense (i.e., it follows a logical chain of thought) but that your argument be based on observable truths.

Douglas Groothuis notes[11] that Jesus does not leave the matter only with his assertions but appeals to evidence to which his hearers would have had access. In other words, Jesus didn't just speak in generalities or use semantics to win arguments. He was a fact-based thinker. In the Gospel of John Jesus makes the following statements:

1. John the Baptist, a respected prophet, testified to Jesus' identity (5:31–35).
2. Jesus' miraculous works also testified to his identity (5:36).
3. The Father testified to Jesus' identity (5:37).
4. The Scriptures likewise testified to his identity (5:39).
5. Moses testified to who Jesus is (5:46).

[11]Groothuis, "Jesus: Philosopher and Apologist."

While it is certainly valid for people to test the validity of these facts (indeed, complicated and long-fought battles have been waged on each), the passages clearly show that Jesus had an appreciation for appeals to evidence, that he understood the importance of fact-based thinking. Evidence is one of the critical elements of logos that you can implement in daily communications.

In your office, this may translate into building the case for a key business decision before you make a presentation. Load your presentations with survey data, financial results, and quantitative analysis where possible—people will respect your diligence in gathering the facts and will feel more at ease because of hard numbers that support your decisions. When dealing with fuzzier concepts such as human perception, use survey results or focus group data to reinforce your points; and employ case studies (historical examples of other companies or products facing a similar situation) to ground your assertions in evidence.

At home, don't just complain to your spouse about vague issues. Give him or her examples of behavior that bothers you ("Last week you left the toilet seat up five times," "We haven't been to a movie in three weeks"), so that your protests are concrete and easy for your mate to remedy and understand.

By introducing evidence to an argument, you make that argument easier to grasp and give it firmer support in truth. By requiring evidence in the arguments of others, you assure that they've spent the time to think through their points and that they have the facts necessary to support them.[12]

CUMULATIVE CASE: GIVE YOUR CONCLUSION MORE THAN ONE LEG TO STAND ON

Finally, while there are a number of other useful logical tools employed by Jesus, one that applies to all forms of logical argumentation is the importance of developing a cumulative case to support your conclusions.

[12]One other important element of the appeal to evidence is that it be an appeal to *credible* evidence. Not all sources of fact are created equal. Most people hold certain sources to be more reputable, and hence more powerful in persuasion, than others. We will review the importance of credibility in the subsequent chapter on ethos.

By now, we are acquainted with the basic syllogistic structure, which is just a chain of logical thought.

SYLLOGISTIC ARGUMENT STRUCTURE

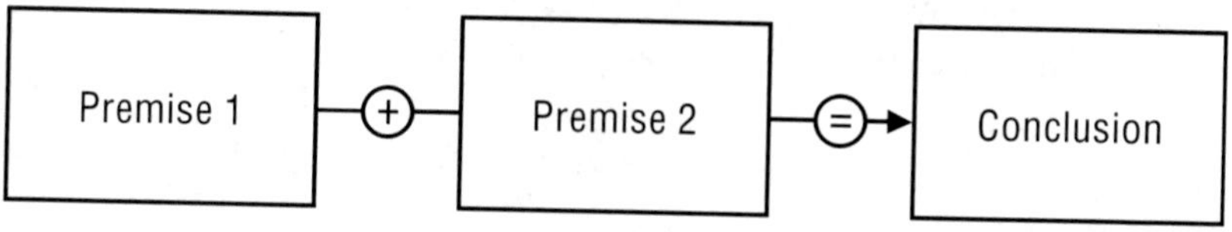

Just as important as proper structure and reason, however, is the principle supporting your conclusions in multiple ways. You might think of building the cumulative case as giving your argument multiple legs.

MULTIPLE SUPPORTS

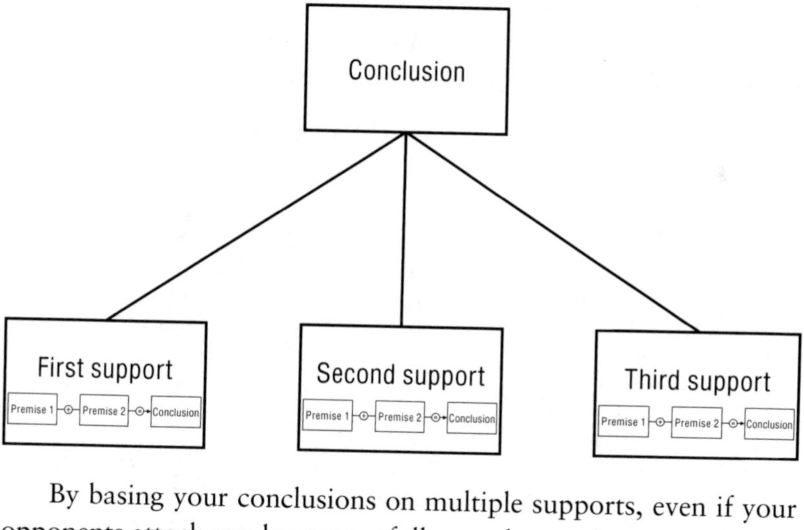

By basing your conclusions on multiple supports, even if your opponents attack one leg successfully, you have other supports that maintain the truth of your conclusion; and, more broadly, most people find a conclusion with multiple supports more generally compelling than one with only one support.

Jesus understood this principle. As in the previous example from the Gospel of John, Jesus did not supply one fact or argument to prove his divinity but many:

1. John the Baptist, a respected prophet, testified to Jesus' identity (5:31–35).
2. Jesus' miraculous works also testified to his identity (5:36).
3. The Father testified to Jesus' identity (5:37).
4. The Scriptures likewise testified to his identity (5:39).
5. Moses testified to who Jesus is (5:46).

By doing so, Jesus made his argument both more compelling and more resistant to attack.

Where possible, always ground your conclusions on as many arguments and facts as possible. We are all fallible, and the more evidence we add to a case, the more likely we will arrive at true conclusions.

CONCLUSION

Again, this chapter is not a full accounting of ways in which we can cultivate logos, nor is it a comprehensive list of the ways Jesus employed logic in his communication. But it does serve two important purposes. First, it shows that as a man Jesus was extremely concerned with being logical, as evidenced by his sophisticated use of logic as a tool of persuasion. He understood reason as a part of human nature and employed it consistently in his communication. For centuries great Christian thinkers like Thomas Aquinas and Blaise Pascal pushed Christians to better understand the role of reason in the Christian faith and to recognize that the logic implicit in the life of Christ is part of the very nature of the world in which we live. Maintaining that legacy of reason and fact-based thinking in Christian thought is essential to maintaining our focus on truth. We hope this is a small contribution to sustaining that legacy. Second, this chapter should give you an initial platform for the exploration of logic in your day-to-day communication with believers and nonbelievers alike.

As a side note, in his *Art of Rhetoric* Aristotle described logos as more than just reason or logical argumentation. For the philosopher, logos entailed both thought and action. Jesus proved to be an exemplar, combining impeccable reasoning with a logically consistent behavior. As Cardinal Joseph Ratzinger, now Pope Benedict XVI, once noted, "Christianity must always remember that it is the religion of the 'Logos.'"[13] For Christians, logic isn't merely confined to argumentation—it extends to action. And while we can benefit immensely from modeling Jesus' reasoning techniques, to be truly effective in applying logic we must remember to mimic the way he lived his life.

[13]Pope Benedict XVI (Joseph Ratzinger), *Christianity and the Crisis of Cultures* (Ft. Collins, CO: Ignatius Press, 2006), 49.

CONCEPT REVIEW

Logos: Logical appeal.

Syllogism: A sequence of two statements, called premises, the truth of which implies the truth of a third statement, known as a conclusion.

Enthymeme: An abbreviated and more powerful form of the syllogism in which a premise or conclusion is merely implied.

Syllogismus: The use of a remark or an image that calls upon the audience to draw an obvious conclusion.

A fortiori: A claim we are bound to accept because of our prior acceptance of a weaker application of the same reasoning or truth.

Reductio ad absurdum: A type of logical argument in which one assumes a claim for the sake of argument, derives an absurd or ridiculous outcome, and then concludes that the original assumption must have been wrong, as it led to an absurd result.

False dilemma: A situation in which two alternative points of view are held to be the only options, when in reality there exists one or more other options that have not been considered.

Appeal to evidence: A line of argumentation based on accepted fact.

Cumulative case: A case based on multiple logical supports that can survive without any one given support.

QUESTIONS FOR FURTHER CONSIDERATION

1. Why is it important that Jesus used logic in his communication? What does Jesus' use of logic say about the importance of human reason?
2. How could the church benefit from a deeper recognition of the importance of logos in human communication?
3. In what ways are Christians properly applying logos to public life? In what ways are Christians poorly applying those principles?
4. Where do you most often encounter logos?
5. What forms of argumentation do you encounter the most? What arguments would benefit you most in your communication?
6. What fallacies are you most prone to make? To which fallacies are you most susceptible?

CHAPTER THREE

ETHOS

JESUS AS SHEPHERD, SAVIOR, TEACHER, AND FRIEND

In 1856 murmurs of rebellion against French colonial rule began to spread throughout Algeria. A group of Muslim holy men known as marabouts were able to stir dissent and gain prominence by convincing the local populations that they possessed supernatural powers. The amazing feats of these "god-like" men allowed them to gain considerable influence, which the religious faction planned to use to overthrow their European rulers.

Realizing that something must be done but not wanting to commit more of his exhausted troops to the North African colony, Napoleon III and his Arab Bureau conceived a quirky plan involving "The Father of Modern Magic," Jean Eugene Robert-Houdin. (While you may not have heard of him, you probably do know about the aspiring teenage magician named Ehrich Weiss who renamed himself after his hero as Harry Houdini.)

The conjurer was called out of retirement and sent to Algeria to provide a command performance before a gathering of superstitious Arab chieftains. Setting up in a theater in the capital city of Algiers, the French magician performed astounding stunts—catching a bullet being fired by an audience member, making a young Arab disappear, and, with the ingenious use of an electromagnet, stripping the strength of a muscular man who was unable to lift a metal box.

The crowds, certain that they were in the presence of Satan, grew fearful of the French sorcerer. But then Robert-Houdin broke the magician's cardinal rule: he sent out translators to explain how the tricks were done. The stunned Arabs realized that they had been duped, not only by the Frenchman but by the marabouts. The holy men lost credibility, and the revolution was averted.

Intuitively we realize that the credibility of a communicator is almost as important as the message he delivers. In this way, a person's credibility on a particular message becomes part of the message itself. The marabouts were trusted because they seemed to possess magical powers. We listen to pastors because they have taken the time to study the Bible and they attempt to lead godly lives, and we trust a CEO when he has a record of positive decision-making. Aristotle called this concept of credibility "ethos."

"Ethos is the persuasive appeal of one's character, and especially how this character is established by means of the speech or discourse."[1] To put it more simply, ethos is argument by character. Against the views of some of his contemporaries, Aristotle believed that personal goodness contributed heavily to a rhetor's overall persuasive ability. Indeed, Aristotle argued, "character is almost so to speak, the controlling factor in persuasion."[2]

Jesus, of course, relied heavily on his credibility as a communicator. He was an exemplar of ethos. Whether performing miracles to prove his connection with the divine, living a sinless life, reciting the old Scriptures, or practicing what he preached, Christ took the time to build credibility with his audiences and used that ethos to add influence to his message. From his character and the means he used to build it, we can draw critical conclusions about the ways in which Christ constructed his own ethos and how that is applicable to us as we engage in our own communications.

CATEGORIES OF ETHOS

Unlike logos and pathos, ethos is a property of communication that belongs not to the speaker but to the audience. The listener, rather than the rhetor, determines whether the speaker's ethos is high or low.

[1]"Silva Rhetoricae"; rhetoric.byu.edu/.
[2]Aristotle, *On Rhetoric*, trans. George A. Kennedy (New York: Oxford University Press: 1991).

Aristotle outlined three categories of ethos that, if followed in speaking situations, could help develop a high ethos:

Phronesis—practical skills and wisdom.

Arête—virtue and goodness.

Eunoia—goodwill toward the audience.

We will explore these categories specifically, outlining their prevalence in the rhetoric of Christ before exploring a number of other ways in which Jesus constructed personal credibility to enhance the power of his communications.

PHRONESIS: THE WISDOM OF COMMON SENSE

Phronesis is the ability to think about how and why we should act in order to change things, and especially to change our lives for the better. According to Aristotle, phronesis isn't simply a skill since it involves not only the ability to decide how to achieve a certain end, but also the ability to reflect upon and determine that end. In rhetoric, phronesis encompasses practical wisdom or common sense. If you have it, people will respect your judgment; if you do not, they will find you less persuasive.

Aristotle claims that the acquisition of *phronesis* requires time, as one must gain both the habit and understanding of correct deliberation:

> [W]hile young men become geometricians and mathematicians and wise in matters like these, it is thought that a young man of practical wisdom cannot be found. The cause is that such wisdom is concerned not only with universals but with particulars, which become familiar from experience, but a young man has no experience, for it is length of time that gives experience.[3]

And again:

> *Phronesis* is concerned with particulars, because it is concerned with how to act in particular situations. One can learn the prin-

[3]Aristotle, *Nicomachean Ethics*; http://www.martinfrost.ws/htmlfiles/nicomachean_part2.html.

ciples of action, but applying them in the real world, in situations one could not have foreseen, requires experience of the world.[4]

A particularly amusing example of someone using *phronesis* to raise his ethos can be found in Aristotle's *Politics*. He relates how Thales the Milesian was mocked for his poverty because he spent all his time on philosophy, which his detractors declared was of little practical use. In response Thales used his knowledge of meteorology to forecast a bumper crop of olives and then used his meager finances to rent out all the olive presses in the area. When the harvest came in, he was able to charge exorbitant rates for use of the presses, making him extremely wealthy in less than a year. According to Aristotle, Thales had "convinced them that it was easy for philosophers to be rich if they chose it, but that that was not what they aimed at; in this manner is Thales said to have shown his wisdom."[5]

One of the most useful of all practical skills is the ability to wisely apply the Word of God to everyday life. Not surprisingly, Jesus is unsurpassed as a model for Scripture application. The religious leaders of his day often learned of his ability at the expense of their own ethos, as is evident in John 8:2–11:

> Early in the morning he came again to the temple. All the people came to him, and he sat down and taught them. The scribes and the Pharisees brought a woman who had been caught in adultery, and placing her in the midst they said to him, "Teacher, this woman has been caught in the act of adultery. Now in the Law Moses commanded us to stone such women. So what do you say?" This they said to test him, that they might have some charge to bring against him.
>
> Jesus bent down and wrote with his finger on the ground. And as they continued to ask him, he stood up and said to them, "Let him who is without sin among you be the first to throw a stone at her." And once more he bent down and wrote on the ground. But when they heard it, they went away one by one, beginning with the older ones, and Jesus was left alone with the woman standing before him.

[4]See http://en.wikipedia.org/wiki/Phronesis.
[5]See http://aristotle.thefreelibrary.com/A-Treatise-on-Government/1-11, excerpted from Book 1, Chapter XI of Aristotle's *Politics* (also known as "A Treatise on Government").

> Jesus stood up and said to her, "Woman, where are they? Has no one condemned you?" She said, "No one, Lord." And Jesus said, "Neither do I condemn you; go, and from now on sin no more."

Most commentary on this passage focuses on the clever way in which Jesus resolved the situation. Hidden within this passage, however, is a curious, often overlooked line about the response by the religious leaders: "But when they heard it, they went away one by one, *beginning with the older ones*" (emphasis added).

Why did the older scribes and Pharisees walk away first? Perhaps, as Aristotle noted, since younger people often lack practical wisdom they are less likely to recognize that deficit than are their elders. The old men were quick to recognize that Jesus had won the argument.

The reason this is worth noting is because it serves as a reminder that the reaction of the audience will not necessarily be uniform. Even in this scene we find that Jesus is being heard by five distinct types of listeners:

- his disciples
- the other people in the Temple (some of whom were followers, others who were not)
- the scribes and Pharisees
- the adulterous woman
- the Heavenly Father

Each person would have assigned a higher or lower ranking to Jesus' ethos based on what values they believed he shared with them. The scribes and Pharisees valued legalism and thought they could trap Jesus by showing that he did not share their high opinion of God's Law. The adulterous woman, who needed forgiveness, would naturally value mercy. The disciples and other people in the Temple were likely to have conflicted views, unsure of whether justice or mercy should take precedence. Jesus' response proved that he was able to reflect upon and determine the best course of action for *this particular situation* in a way that exhibited perfect *phronesis*.

Just as Jesus was able to show that he shared his audience's values, we need to be able to show that we sympathize with our hearers' feelings and concerns in order to be persuasive. In doing so, however, we must also remember that, like Jesus, our first and most important audience is the Heavenly Father.

Empathy with the audience, however, is not the only part of the trust equation. As Jay Heinrichs points out:

> When you share your audience's values, they believe you will apply them to whatever choice you help them make. If evangelical Protestants think you want to do what Jesus would do, they probably will find you trustworthy. If an environmentalist considers you earth-centric, she will respect your thinking about the proposed new power plant. But sharing your values is not sufficient. They also have to believe that you know the right thing to do at the particular moment. While an evangelical Christian will respect you for trying to do what Jesus would do, he still won't let you remove his appendix.[6]

So far we have mainly examined wise application in particular situations. But as Heinrichs notes, the audience should not only consider you a sensible and trustworthy person, but sufficiently knowledgeable to deal with the problem at hand. "When you remove an appendix, a medical degree proves your practical wisdom more than your knowledge of the Bible."[7]

Several years ago the hotel chain Holiday Inn Express produced several humorous television commercials consisting of average people performing extraordinary activities that only experts would know. One ad begins on a skydiving plane. A man who appears to be an instructor stands at an open door guiding first-time jumpers. "Give me a clean exit and a good arch, go!" he yells. The diver jumps as others follow out the door. The man again yells, "Pay attention, right, heads up, at 4,500 feet look, reach, pull. Go, come on, you can do it." The divers jump while listening to his instruction. A woman about to jump stops and asks the man, "How many times have you done this?" He answers, "None, but I just stayed at

[6]Jay Heinrichs, *Thank You for Arguing* (New York: Three Rivers Press, 2007), 67.
[7]Ibid.

a Holiday Inn Express last night." The woman dives out the door. The commercial cuts to a black screen with the message, "It won't make you smarter. But you'll feel smarter."

While you may be able to initially fool an audience, feeling smarter is no substitute for actual expertise. When jumping out of a plane for the first time we prefer to have someone with real-world experience, not just someone who got a good night's sleep.

ARÊTE: A DEDICATION TO EXCELLENCE

In its basic sense *arête* means "goodness," "excellence," or "virtue" of any kind. Aristotle used it to refer to the fulfillment of purpose or function, the act of living up to one's full potential. That philosopher recognized that one key component of effective ethos is a general dedication to excellence in one's life.

Jesus was both an exemplar and a proponent of excellence, particularly the kind of excellence associated with moral virtue. Although nothing is known about his skills as a carpenter in the years preceding his ministry, much is said of Christ's excellence in miracles and ministry.

As an example, when Christ performed his first miracle—turning water into wine at the wedding in Cana—the resulting wine was heralded as the best of the party. After tasting it, the master of the banquet exclaimed, "Everyone serves the good wine first, and when people have drunk freely, then the poor wine. But you have kept the good wine until now" (John 2:10).

In ministry, Christ demonstrated excellence of both personal moral character and spiritual discipline. His knowledge of the Scriptures was unparalleled. He discussed the Torah with experts in the Temple as a child, and his knowledge of the Torah later in life won him the title "rabbi" (teacher) and allowed him to converse freely and knowledgeably with the Pharisees and religious leaders. The term for this rhetorical strategy is *anamnesis*, calling to memory past matters—specifically, citing a past author from memory.

Although he lived in a culture with a strong oral tradition, Jesus proved to be exceptionally adept at recalling Scripture from memory. He quoted from twenty-four of the thirty-nine books of the Old Testament and used the phrase "it is written" almost sixty times when quoting Scripture. His knowledge was remarkable, considering he was only a "carpenter's son" (Matthew 13:53–56).

Anamnesis helps establish ethos since it conveys the idea that the speaker is knowledgeable of the received wisdom from the past. And the crowds were astonished at Jesus' teaching, for he was teaching them as one who had authority, unlike their scribes (Matthew 7:28–29). This is yet another reason why Christians should follow Jesus' example by memorizing Scripture.

Similarly, his followers could trust that he also possessed moral excellence. The story of Christ's temptation in the wilderness (Matthew 4:1–11; Mark 1:12–13; Luke 4:1–13) proved his discipline and moral irreproachability. On every front—moral, intellectual, interpersonal, and others—Christ's followers could count on his excellence, and that *arête* bought him enormous credibility and trust.

Furthermore, those in the Christian tradition are encouraged to display a similar *arête* in their own lives. First Corinthians 9:24 reminds followers, "Do you not know that in a race all the runners run, but only one receives the prize? So run that you may obtain it." And other passages such as Philippians 4:8 remind the disciples of Christ that they are called to excellence in everything that might be termed a virtue:

> Finally, brothers, whatever is true, whatever is honorable, whatever is just, whatever is pure, whatever is lovely, whatever is commendable, if there is any excellence, if there is anything worthy of praise, think about these things.

Do you focus on excellence in every part of your life? As a Christian witness, are you both strong in your faith and knowledgeable about the Scriptures and religious life? Can you speak intelligently on your religion, or do you often find yourself "stuck" in conversations with those who disagree with you?

In a broader context, are you a good employee, father, friend, neighbor? Do you spend time improving your mind and treat your body as a temple, or do you spend your free time in trivial pursuits?

We don't often think about *arête*, but moral excellence is a major way in which we communicate our seriousness and trustworthiness to others. As Aristotle noted, ethos is not only related to your credibility on the specific subject about which you are speaking but also to your general moral character. To improve your effectiveness as a rhetor, work first on improving your character.

EUNOIA: COURTING GOODWILL

Eunoia is the feeling of friendship and goodwill that is evoked by the rhetor. As defined by Aristotle, *eunoia* is an element of both pathos and ethos. It is the cultivation through appearance, word, and action of goodwill toward the audience, generating a feeling in them that you are trustworthy and have their best interest in mind. *Eunoia* can include visual elements such as physical appearance—clothes, stance, and posture. It is best cultivated through word and action, generating meaningful, benevolent relationships with the audience and its individual members.

Jesus was a master of *eunoia*. Whereas the religious authorities of his day refused to commiserate with the common people, Jesus spent his time with beggars, prostitutes, and tax collectors. He healed those who were sick and suffering and even brought the dead back to life. He fed those who were hungry and gave hope to those in despair. He also condemned those who made life difficult for the common people of Israel. Where other Jews condemned Samaritans, he gained credibility with them by working with this outcast group.

Throughout his ministry Jesus' message was one of hope and deliverance for the common people of the world. As John 3:17 says, "God did not send his Son into the world to condemn the world, but in order that the world might be saved through him." On multiple occasions Jesus encouraged all believers to help the poor and less fortunate among them. Speaking in Matthew 25:40 (through a parable), Jesus says, "And the King will answer them, 'Truly, I say to you, as you did it to one of the least of these my brothers, you did it to me.'" At its foundation, Jesus' message was one of hope, understanding, forgiveness, and deliverance for the common people, sinners, and social outcasts, and his dogged determinism to fight for those groups made Jesus a hero to many of the downtrodden in his society. This focus on their needs and concerns increased his credibility and influence with them.

Many pastors, politicians, and businesspeople take a similar approach in building their ethos. When Bill Clinton said, "I feel your pain," he was creating a sense of empathy and goodwill with his audience. When Mother Teresa took the time to work with the poor, sick, and outcast of Calcutta she generated enormous *eunoia* not only with the people of India but with others around the world. When Wal-Mart sent truckloads of supplies into New Orleans after Hurricane Katrina, the company gained credibility with the people of Louisiana and others around the country by showing that it had their best interest in mind. Likewise, Christians across the world generate an enormous amount of goodwill by volunteering at soup kitchens, setting up free health-care clinics, building schools in impoverished areas, and delivering food and supplies to areas of the world ravaged by disease and war.

What are you doing as a communicator to establish your *eunoia*? Are you taking the time to build goodwill with the people with whom you communicate? When at work, do you get to know your employees, give them your time, and mentor them, or do you simply issue orders and directives? At school, do you spend extra time with students who are struggling, or does your workday end when the bell rings at 3:00 P.M.? Pastors, are you really there for your parishioners, or are you just a face on Sunday that is uninvolved the rest of the week? When you speak to an audience, do you take the time to show them how your proposals will work to their benefit, or do you simply focus on the genius of your solutions?

Eunoia is difficult to build. It is often ambiguous, and it takes care to maintain. But audience goodwill is essential if you want to communicate effectively and persuasively.

BOASTING: PROCLAIMING YOURSELF

Boasting or bragging is one of the most obvious ways to establish authority with one's audience. We are all experts on ourselves and tend to know more about our own strengths and virtues (whether real or imagined) than anyone else. Unfortunately, bragging can backfire. Often such boasting is rightly seen as a sign of pride and immodesty.

One notable exception from Scripture comes from the book of Job. Job lost his property, children, and health. After several rounds of debate between him and his friends over why he was being punished, God answered Job "out of the whirlwind" (Job 38:1):

> *"Where were you when I laid the foundation of the earth?*
> *Tell me, if you have understanding.*
> *Who determined its measurements—surely you know!*
> *Or who stretched the line upon it?*
> *On what were its bases sunk,*
> *or who laid its cornerstone,*
> *when the morning stars sang together*
> *and all the sons of God shouted for joy?" (Job 38:4–7)*

After this line of questioning was completed, Job answered God:

> *"Behold, I am of small account; what shall I answer you?*
> *I lay my hand on my mouth.*
> *I have spoken once, and I will not answer;*
> *twice, but I will proceed no further." (Job 40:4–5)*

The ethos of Jehovah trumped the ethos of Job!

As Jay Heinrichs notes, "You don't mess with God's ethos. He has virtue to spare; in fact, he *constitutes* virtue." He adds, "reciting your resumé is not the most effective way to enhance your ethos."[8] In general, do not boast or brag.

Consider the example provided by Jesus. Though he was the Son of God, heralded as Messiah, rabbi, and prophet by his followers on earth, he was never immodest or boastful. Philippians 2:5–8 speaks for itself:

> Have this mind among yourselves, which is yours in Christ Jesus, who, though he was in the form of God, did not count equality with God a thing to be grasped, but made himself nothing, taking

[8]Ibid., 69.

> the form of a servant, being born in the likeness of men. And being found in human form, he humbled himself by becoming obedient to the point of death, even death on a cross.

As Christians, we should model the humility of Christ. Rather than boasting or bragging, use self-reporting and character references or witnesses to enhance your credibility.

SELF-REPORTING: RECITING YOUR QUALIFICATIONS

A distinction can be drawn between boasting (talking in a self-admiring way) and self-reporting (humbly listing your qualifications). "Reciting your resumé" is not a substitute for establishing ethos, but it can establish a foundation for why the audience should listen to you. The difference between boasting and self-reporting is not merely a matter of how meek you are in establishing your credentials. The context also determines when it is applicable. Pointing out that you have a PhD in theology can be relevant self-reporting when applying for a teaching position at a Christian college, but it may be mere bragging when speaking to your son's Little League team.

List your credentials on relevant subject-matter expertise when it is relevant to the topic about which you are speaking. But don't overdo it. Let your expertise come through in your presentation rather than in your self-report.

CHARACTER REFERENCES/WITNESSES

A more effective means of establishing your virtue is to have someone else—preferably someone with high ethos—do the bragging for you. The Gospels record that at the beginning of Jesus' ministry, he went down to the Jordan River to be baptized by his cousin John. At the time in first-century Palestine, there was probably no person of higher ethos than John the Baptist. Although he had the appearance (he wore a garment of camel's hair and a leather belt around his waist) and behavior (he ate locusts and wild honey) of a wild man, he was acknowledged to be a prophet, "he who was spoken of by the prophet Isaiah" (Matthew 3:3).

> The next day he saw Jesus coming toward him, and said, "Behold, the Lamb of God, who takes away the sin of the world! This is he of whom I said, 'After me comes a man who ranks before me, because he was before me.' I myself did not know him, but for this purpose I came baptizing with water, that he might be revealed to Israel." And John bore witness: "I saw the Spirit descend from heaven like a dove, and it remained on him. I myself did not know him, but he who sent me to baptize with water said to me, 'He on whom you see the Spirit descend and remain, this is he who baptizes with the Holy Spirit.' And I have seen and have borne witness that this is the Son of God." (John 1:29–34)

It is easy for the modern reader to miss the significance of this event. From our historical vantage point, Jesus is the one with the highest ethos. He needs no introduction. Yet those who were standing on the banks of the Jordan that day would have viewed the situation completely differently. To that audience John the Baptist, a prophet of God, was a man of the highest virtue and goodwill. For him to claim that another of even higher ethos was in their presence would have been an extraordinary character reference.

An example of the effect that John's words had on his audience can be found in John 1:35–37:

> The next day again John was standing with two of his disciples, and he looked at Jesus as he walked by and said, "Behold, the Lamb of God!" The two disciples heard him say this, and they followed Jesus.

Neither of the two men, one of which was Andrew, Simon Peter's brother, knew about Jesus. But they did know John the Baptist and as his disciples held him in high esteem. For him to praise Jesus in such a manner was enough to convince them of his ethos and their need to follow him.

This is a powerful biblical concept. Look at any book jacket or cover and you will see it in action. Authors often court high-profile individuals to endorse their books with short quotes of support on the cover. Movies often list top reviews or Oscar nominations on their posters and advertisements. Speakers almost never begin their speeches with their own accomplishments. Instead they have someone introduce them and speak of those accomplishments on their behalf, enhancing their credibility without sacrificing their humility.

In your own communications, seek to enhance your rhetoric through character references and witnesses rather than through boasting or self-reporting. When giving a speech or presentation, have someone introduce you, hitting the high points of your qualifications. In interpersonal relationships, frequently speak up on behalf of others; in doing so, you will find that they are more inclined to speak up for you. And if you have witnesses, seek in every way possible to bolster their credibility. Jesus seemed to affirm John's status as a prophet by seeking him out for baptism. Affirm the credibility of your own witnesses, and you will enhance your own credibility as well.

TACTICAL FLAW: MAKING YOURSELF REAL

In his book *Thank You for Arguing*, Jay Heinrichs proposes that an effective means of establishing ethos is to reveal a personal tactical flaw, a weakness that wins sympathy or shows the sacrifice you have made for the audience.

In the spring of 1783 the finances of the United States were in disarray, leaving Congress without the funds to pay the army. A group of soldiers among the officer corps stationed with George Washington on the Hudson River grew mutinous. There was even talk of a military coup d'état. To quell such talk Washington gathered the officers in an assembly and established common ground with his audience by reminding them of the experiences they had shared. In his speech the general reminded his officers of his faithfulness to them and to the cause:

> If my conduct heretofore, has not evinced to you, that I have been a faithful friend to the Army, my declaration of it at this moment wd. be equally unavailing and improper. But as I was among the first who embarked in the cause of our common Country. As I have never left your side one moment, but when called from you on public duty. As I have been the constant companion and witness of

> your Distresses, and not among the last to feel, and acknowledge your Merits. As I have ever considered my own Military reputation as inseparably connected with that of the Army. As my Heart has ever expanded with joy, when I have heard its praises, and my indignation has arisen, when the mouth of detraction has been opened against it, it can scarcely be supposed, at this late stage of the War, that I am indifferent to its interests.[9]

His words alone might have been enough to sway the crowd. But Washington, a theatergoer since the age of nineteen, had a flair for the theatrical. He pulled a letter from Congress out of his pocket and fussed with it, as if he were unable to read the words. Finally he pulled on a pair of eyeglasses and said, "Gentlemen, you will permit me to put on my spectacles, for I have not only grown gray but almost blind in the service of my country."

The officers, a cadre of battle-hardened soldiers, broke into tears. After Washington left the hall, the meeting voted unanimously "that the officers reciprocated his affectionate expressions with the greatest sincerity of which the human heart is capable."[10] By showing a tactical weakness—and reminding his men of his ethos—Washington had averted the coup. As the British historian Paul Johnson contends, "One is tempted to say it was Washington's finest hour."[11]

Benjamin Rush observed that Washington "has so much martial dignity in his deportment that you would distinguish him to be a general and a soldier from among 10,000 people. There is not a king in Europe that would not look like a *valet de chambre* by his side."[12] Another admirer was Joseph Reed, a young lawyer who was chosen to be part of an escort accompanying Washington on a trip from Philadelphia to New York. Reed was so smitten by the general that he signed on to be Washington's secretary. As he explained, Washington had "expressed himself to me in such terms that I thought myself bound by every tie of duty and

[9]"Speech to the Officers of the Army, Head Quarters, Newburgh, March 15, 1783"; http://www.pbs.org/georgewashington/milestones/newburgh_read.html.
[10]Richard Brookhiser, *Founding Father: Rediscovering George Washington* (New York: The Free Press, 1996), 45.
[11]Paul Johnson, *George Washington: The Founding Father* (New York: HarperCollins, 2005), 77.
[12]David McCullough, *1776* (New York: Simon & Schuster, 2005), 43.

honor to comply with his request to help him through the sea of difficulties."[13]

Neither logos nor pathos is likely to inspire that level of instant devotion.

Washington's theatrics provide an exemplary case of the first definition of the tactical flaw: showing weakness that wins sympathy with the audience. What made the gesture persuasive was that it helped to humanize Washington and played on his officers' love and sympathy for what he had sacrificed. No doubt some of them understood that the action was done for rhetorical effect; yet they were moved because it was believable. If it had been phony it could have backfired, causing the general to lose a bit of his ethos.

Although there are no instances in which Jesus used weakness to win sympathy, the Gospels do provide an archetypical example of the second meaning: showing the sacrifice one has made for the audience.

> Jesus, knowing that the Father had given all things into his hands, and that he had come from God and was going back to God, rose from supper. He laid aside his outer garments, and taking a towel, tied it around his waist. Then he poured water into a basin and began to wash the disciples' feet and to wipe them with the towel that was wrapped around him. He came to Simon Peter, who said to him, "Lord, do you wash my feet?" Jesus answered him, "What I am doing you do not understand now, but afterward you will understand." Peter said to him, "You shall never wash my feet." Jesus answered him, "If I do not wash you, you have no share with me." Simon Peter said to him, "Lord, not my feet only but also my hands and my head!" Jesus said to him, "The one who has bathed does not need to wash, except for his feet, but is completely clean. And you are clean, but not every one of you." For he knew who was to betray him; that was why he said, "Not all of you are clean."
>
> When he had washed their feet and put on his outer garments and resumed his place, he said to them, "Do you understand what I have done to you? You call me Teacher and Lord, and you are right, for so I am. If I then, your Lord and Teacher, have washed your feet, you also ought to wash one another's feet. For I have given you an

---

[13]Ibid., 44.

> example, that you also should do just as I have done to you. Truly, truly, I say to you, a servant is not greater than his master, nor is a messenger greater than the one who sent him. If you know these things, blessed are you if you do them." (John 13:3–17)

At this point in his ministry it would have been sufficient for Jesus to merely tell his disciples that he expected them to serve others. His credibility was so firmly established that they would have felt compelled to listen to any admonitions he gave them. Rather than relying merely on words, though, Jesus used an argument from character. If their Master—the very Son of God—was willing to kneel before them and wipe the dust from their feet, how much more should they feel compelled to do the same for others.

Admit your weaknesses, and show humility in your interactions with others. We distrust those who seem too perfect because we know that no one on earth is without flaw. We become frustrated with those who seem overly confident or knowledgeable because they seem to be hiding something. You might be surprised by how effective it can be to admit weaknesses or to use that taboo phrase, "I don't know."

BORROWED CREDIBILITY: CONSULTING SOURCES

In the chapter on logos, we discussed the necessity of appeals to evidence in rational communication. It is important to base your arguments on facts, and some measure of research or outside knowledge is often necessary to accumulate those facts. However, with relation to logical argumentation, facts are only useful if they come from credible sources. In turn, if you have limited authority on a particular subject or if your reputation has yet to form with your audience, you can borrow the credibility of the sources you cite.

This is easy to see in the world around us. *The New York Times* is known as "the newspaper of record" in the United States because it is deemed a reliable source of information on numerous topics. If I am speaking on a subject, citing the *Times* can heighten the credibility of my argument. It can grant ethos to that argument even when people are unfamiliar with my character because the *Times* has established character—and a record of truthful reporting—that grants it special status as a source of credible information. Similarly, even when people doubt my own credibility, they are likely to accept the arguments I cite by well-known, respected speakers, thinkers, publications, or data sources. I am, in essence, borrowing the credibility of those people or sources.

Jesus used this method by quoting Scripture and the words of well-known prophets. When tempted by Satan in the desert, Jesus did not resort to his own argumentation but used the arguments provided him by Scripture. Luke 4:1–13 reads:

> And Jesus, full of the Holy Spirit, returned from the Jordan and was led by the Spirit in the wilderness for forty days, being tempted by the devil. And he ate nothing during those days. And when they were ended, he was hungry. The devil said to him, "If you are the Son of God, command this stone to become bread." And Jesus answered him, "It is written, 'Man shall not live by bread alone.'"
>
> And the devil took him up and showed him all the kingdoms of the world in a moment of time, and said to him, "To you I will give all this authority and their glory, for it has been delivered to me, and I give it to whom I will. If you, then, will worship me, it will all be yours." And Jesus answered him, "It is written, 'You shall worship the Lord your God, and him only shall you serve.'"
>
> And he took him to Jerusalem and set him on the pinnacle of the temple and said to him, "If you are the Son of God, throw yourself down from here, for it is written, 'He will command his angels concerning you, to guard you,' and "'On their hands they will bear you up, lest you strike your foot against a stone.'"
>
> And Jesus answered him, "It is said, 'You shall not put the Lord your God to the test.'" And when the devil had ended every temptation, he departed from him until an opportune time.

Time and again Christ relies not on his own authority but on the authority of his sources, in this case God as revealed through Old Testament Scripture—a source having great authority with Satan and with the people of Israel (specifically the Pharisees) with whom Christ communicated.

When you are assembling a case, don't just think about the logic of the facts you are assembling; think about the credibility of your sources. This is particularly important if you do not have a positive preexisting reputation with your audience or if you are speaking on a subject about which you have little experience. Even when you lack ethos, you can borrow the ethos of those sources and thereby reinforce your own credibility.

If you are a teacher working with kids, cite sources from popular culture that they respect, and they may grant you credibility for your familiarity with material they find credible. If you are a pastor, cite sources that your local audience respects—local politicians or sports heroes, other pastors, or prominent local publications—that show you are both in touch with that particular group and with the most credible sources on the subject about which you are speaking. If you are making a political argument in a campaign speech or a newspaper letter to the editor, call out the sources for the facts you cite—such as *The New York Times*, the National Bureau of Economic Research, or the State Department—and borrow on the established credibility of those institutions. Just because you lack ethos on a subject doesn't mean you can't build ethos on that subject by addressing it with credible facts.

CONCEPT REVIEW

Ethos: The persuasive appeal of one's character, especially how this character is established by means of the speech or discourse.

Phronesis: The ability to think about how and why we should act in order to change things, and especially to change our lives for the better; common sense.

Arête: Fulfillment of purpose or function, especially the act of living up to one's full potential; moral excellence.

Eunoia: The feeling of friendship and goodwill that is evoked by the rhetor.

Anamnesis: Calling to memory past matters; specifically, citing a past author from memory.

Boasting: Talking in a self-admiring way.

Self-reporting: Listing qualifications that are necessary to establish your credibility with your audience.

Character references/witnesses: Having another person list your qualifications for your audience.

Tactical flaw: Revealing a weakness that wins sympathy or shows the sacrifice you have made for the audience.

Borrowed credibility: Using sources to enhance your credibility on a topic for a given audience.

QUESTIONS FOR FURTHER CONSIDERATION

1. What practical skill or knowledge best exemplifies your own phronesis? List three ways in which you might highlight that for your audience.
2. Which public speakers do you most admire for their *arête* (moral excellence)? How are you able to recognize their moral qualities without knowing them personally? How are they able to communicate it through their presentations?
3. Consider how you might present your credentials without boasting. How would you humbly communicate your greatest accomplishments for an audience?
4. Can you recognize examples of tactical flaws by presenters? How would you use this strategy to increase your own ethos?

CHAPTER FOUR

NARRATIVE AND IMAGERY

THE STORY AND STORIES OF A SAVIOR

For the better part of the twentieth century, the world was locked in a battle between two political systems—the democracy of the United States and Western Europe and the Communism of the Soviet Union and China. The battles between these two systems were first waged by philosophers and economists such as John Locke and Karl Marx. They were fought on paper, on battlefields (such as Vietnam), and by the economies of the respective country groups; but they were also punctuated by great storytellers. Stalin capitalized on a burgeoning ideology with class rhetoric and a revolution in Russia. Western politicians such as Margaret Thatcher and Ronald Reagan eventually rose to power based on their ability to simplify the battle and express its moral elements clearly, using the power of imagery and narrative to criticize the failings of "the evil empire." But the Soviet Union itself produced its most moving and inspired critic, author Aleksandr Solzhenitsyn.

A true son of Russia, Solzhenitsyn was raised by his poor widowed mother, a shorthand typist in the town of Rostov. As a child, young Aleksandr was always interested in literature and wrote his own fiction. But Rostov's university didn't offer a proper literary education, and young Aleksandr could not leave due to his mother's poor health and his family's modest circumstances; so he studied mathematics.

In 1945, as Soviet Communism was falling like a cloud over Russia and Eastern Europe, Solzhenitsyn was arrested for writing ill of Stalin in a private letter with a friend and was thrown in a USSR concentration camp for eight years. From that point forward,

Solzhenitsyn cycled through the Soviet "gulags" and in and out of exile, using the stories he gained from his experiences to battle Soviet tyranny. From his stay in a concentration camp for political prisoners in Kazakhstan, he created his first major work, *One Day in the Life of Ivan Denisovich*. In the same camp he contracted a brain tumor that almost killed him and served later as the basis for his novel *Cancer Ward*.[1] Initially Solzhenitsyn's writings were given explicit approval by Soviet leader Nikita Khrushchev. But after Khrushchev was ousted in 1964, Solzhenitsyn was denied further Soviet publication rights and increasingly became a high-profile enemy of the political class in the country he still called home.[2]

His writings told the stories of Soviet Communism, building a consistent narrative of the events in that country while simultaneously marking his own arduous journey through exile and the prison camps. Eventually Solzhenitsyn released the monumental work that would win him the Nobel Prize in literature and bring many Western elites to even starker opposition to the Soviet system—*The Gulag Archipelago*. A three-volume work based on historical research, Solzhenitsyn's own experiences in the prison camps, and interviews with 227 other former prisoners, *The Gulag Archipelago* was a literary colossus that elevated Solzhenitsyn to the status of martyr and finally stripped away the flawed moral authority of the Soviet system. Solzhenitsyn—the storyteller and the story—had done what the economists and philosophers had failed to do: he sucked away the moral appeal of Communism by showing the evil and depredation inherent in the system.

He wrote in personal narratives, parables, and allegories and in doing so communicated the complexity of the problems with the Soviet system through the simplicity of human experience.

Flannery O'Connor once commented:

> When you can state the theme of a story, when you can separate it from the story itself, then you can be sure the story is not a very

[1]See *Nobel Lectures, Literature 1968–1980*, editor-in-charge Tore Frängsmyr, editor Sture Allén (Singapore: World Scientific Publishing, 1993).
[2]Chris Steiner, "In Exile Wherever He Goes," *The New York Times*, March 1, 1998.

> good one. The meaning of a story has to be embodied in it, has to be made concrete in it. A story is a way to say something that can't be said any other way, and it takes every word in the story to say what the meaning is.[3]

Ever since Homer crafted the Greek moral system with his epic poems *The Iliad* and *The Odyssey*, human beings have communicated their most important messages through stories. We teach our children moral lessons through Grimms' fairy tales, Berenstain Bears books, and classic tales like *The Little Engine that Could*. Our great moral leaders have consistently battled culture through literature (Mark Twain confronted the inhumanity of racism with *Huckleberry Finn* and Dickens the darkness of industrial Britain with the genius of *Oliver Twist*). Our grandmothers told us parables to guide us as we encounter moral dilemmas, and even in business we remember the greatest lessons through stories.

Of course, no one mastered the narrative as brilliantly as Jesus—so much so that one of its most popular forms, the parable, has become almost synonymous with Christian teaching despite its prevalence around the world. Jesus brought his moral lessons to life with intricate tales and vivid imagery. He cemented his legacy with a compelling personal narrative and gave his followers perspective and motivation by rooting their struggle in the larger biblical narrative of Judaic history. While many teachers spoke only in proverbs and dictums, Jesus knew the importance of storytelling and used it to ignite his followers and radically alter the political and religious structure of the entire world.

So how did a poor Nazarene carpenter use his stories to such monumental effect? So far we have discussed the essential elements of Jesus' communication—pathos, logos, and ethos. But as important as these three pillars was the way Jesus pulled them together—through narrative and imagery. In this chapter we will start by showing how Jesus used imagery, primarily simile and metaphor, to paint vivid pictures for his followers. Then we will move into a discussion of the way in which he used broader narrative forms,

[3]Flannery O'Connor, *Mystery and Manners* (New York: Farrar, Straus and Giroux, 1969), 96.

such as parables, to memorably and succinctly communicate his complex moral lessons.

IMAGERY: SIMILES AND METAPHORS

We are all familiar with the parables of Christ. But at the heart of Christ's rhetoric is something even simpler than the parable or narrative—imagery. Through the use of descriptive language, similes, and metaphors, Christ condensed the power of the parable to two- and three-word descriptions that bring the Scriptures to life and, like enthymemes, excite our imaginations.

These uses of imagery give us a more vivid understanding of the concepts Christ discussed, but they also allow us to fill in the blanks with our own experiences and mental images, drawing us into the conversation. As C. H. Dodd notes in his *Parables of the Kingdom*, "At its simplest the parable is a metaphor or simile drawn from nature or common life, arresting the hearer by its vividness or strangeness, and leaving the mind in sufficient doubt about its precise application to tease it into active thought."[4]

Christ rarely delivered straight lectures. He used imagery; and at the heart of his stories were a few techniques—primarily metaphor and simile—that enlivened his language, excited his listeners, and allowed generations of audiences to more closely connect with his teachings.

Simile

Imagine you are walking through a museum when you come to a room featuring a new exhibit. The name of the exhibit is "The Kingdom of God."

The first room you enter has a dirt floor with a ceiling that rises up for thirty or forty feet. You notice a small placard on the ground, and it says, "A grain of mustard seed." In front of the card, so small that you would have missed it, lies a small seed. Directly behind the seed, though, a large tree rises up, as if planted in the museum's floor. You realize that the chirping of birds is not

[4]C. H. Dodd, *Parables of the Kingdom* (New York: Scribner's, 1961), 5.

canned noise but the songs of real birds who have made their home in that tree.

You ponder the meaning of the exhibit as you move to the adjacent rooms. Many of the rooms merely contain large screens on which strange films are being projected. In some a person discovers pearls in a marketplace or treasures in a field. Some of the films depict mundane jobs—a worker in a vineyard, a farmer sowing seeds, a fisherman casting a fishnet—while others are about a king, settling debts, and hosting wedding banquets.

As you leave the exhibit hall, pondering the meaning of these images, you stop before a sign that reads, "These things are what the Kingdom of heaven is like."

Reading the Gospels provides a similar experience. Instead of finding sculptures, paintings, or films, we discover imagery that develops through similes—word pictures that create a comparison of two unlike things, usually using "like," "as," or "than." Jesus often used similes, particularly when discussing the Kingdom of God. Consider the examples in which Jesus told us what the Kingdom of Heaven is like:

a mustard seed (Matthew 13:31–32; Mark 4:30–32; Luke 13:18–19)
yeast in bread (Matthew 13:33; Luke 13:20–21)
treasure hidden in a field (Matthew 13:44)
a merchant in search of fine pearls (Matthew 13:45–46)
a fishnet thrown into the sea (Matthew 13:47–48)
a master of a house who hires workers for a vineyard (Matthew 20:1–15)
a man who scattered seed on the ground (Mark 4:26–29)
a man who sowed good seed in a field (Matthew 13:24–30)
a king settling an account with his servants (Matthew 18:21–35)
a king preparing a wedding banquet for his son (Matthew 22:1–14)

We are all accustomed to similes. There is no confusion when your wife proclaims, "This room is as cold as ice!" When your neighbor complains that your grass looks "like a bed of weeds," you know it's time to tend the lawn. And when your son's track coach says he is "as slow as molasses," you know your son is going to have a tough time keeping his place on the team. The simile is an expressive comparison between two things, and it is a cornerstone of epic poetry and everyday conversation. But for some reason when we write a formal piece of communication we eschew similes in favor of mere description.

Quarterly earnings aren't falling "like a rock," they're just falling. A hard-working student isn't "as patient as Job," he's just patient. And language, in the process, loses some of its impact. A fundamental tenet of human psychology is that we often think in pictures. We associate new experiences with past experiences, and we seek to connect the verbal with the visual. Christ used similes to hammer home the impact of his words with associated visual imagery; and it was through the use of simile that Jesus and other New Testament figures made explicit, direct connections between the new concepts they addressed and the real-world images their audiences would understand.

In the modern world, not all similes are one-liners. If you are a businessperson, you may notice the importance of anecdotes or, more formally, case studies in the communication of your most effective colleagues. Anecdotes ("This experience is just like the experience I had fifteen years ago at Company X") serve as incredibly succinct comparisons of complex situations from which a reader can draw broad patterns. Case studies highlight these examples in excruciating detail, picking apart complex stories to find specific comparisons. Either way, these are simply more complex similes in the form of parables or narratives that can be remarkably effective communications tools in numerous situations from the boardroom to the pulpit.

You may not always want to be so explicit or so impactful. In the preceding example you may not want to say that quarterly earnings have been falling "like a rock" because your job is on the line and you'd prefer that concept remain abstract. But if the purpose of your rhetoric is to make new concepts powerful and memorable, similes are an effective use of explicit visual imagery.

Metaphor

While Christ used similes to make many useful comparisons, when he wanted to draw an even closer connection between two things he employed another form—metaphor.

A metaphor is a simple statement that compares two separate things by referring to them as one (e.g., "All the world's a stage"). A metaphor, to use the terminology of linguist George Lakoff, consists of a "source domain" and a "target domain." The source domain is the part of the metaphor we already understand, and the target domain is the part the rhetor is seeking to make us understand. In the metaphor "Life is a highway," for example, the target domain (the part the hearer or audience is trying to understand) is "life," while the source domain (the part that we draw upon from our own experience) is "highway." Because we understand not only what a highway is (a man-made path) but also what occurs on it (travel, adventure, discovery, etc.), we are able to create a conceptual "map" of the source-target pairing in a way that increases our understanding of the target. Whereas a simile makes this comparison explicitly using "like" or "as," a metaphor simply associates the two things directly, as if they were one.

A few examples from the Gospels include:

- "I was sent only to the lost sheep of the house of Israel." (Matthew 15:24)
- "But she came and knelt before him, saying, 'Lord, help me.' And he answered, 'It is not right to take the children's bread and throw it to the dogs.'" (Matthew 15:25–26)
- "In the beginning was the Word, and the Word was with God, and the Word was God." (John 1:1, said about Jesus rather than by Jesus)
- "You serpents, you brood of vipers . . ." (Matthew 23:33, Jesus, speaking to the Pharisees)

As these examples demonstrate, metaphor can be a stronger tool than simile because it does more than compare two things or ideas. It refers to them as equivalent or the same. When Christ said the Pharisees were a "brood of vipers" (rather than "like a brood of vipers"), he was leveling a harsh criticism that dehumanized the Pharisees, making them out to be a writhing group of snakes, figuratively speaking. When John referred to Christ as "the Word," he was saying something more than "Jesus is like the word." He gave us a statement that has been sliced and diced by theologians for centuries for its spiritual importance.

Of course, Jesus isn't the only person to employ metaphor to inspire deeper understanding of a concept or to rouse an audience to action. Some of history's greatest speakers, playwrights, poets, and essayists used metaphors extensively. Consider the Emily Dickinson poem, "XXXII."

HOPE is the thing with feathers
That perches in the soul,
And sings the tune without the words,
And never stops at all,

And sweetest in the gale is heard;
And sore must be the storm
That could abash the little bird
That kept so many warm.

I've heard it in the chillest land,
And on the strangest sea;
Yet, never, in extremity,
It asked a crumb of me.[5]

In her poetry Dickinson used extended metaphors to explore the subtleties of two similar concepts, and here she gives us a deeper understanding of her conception of hope than any 40,000-word tome could. Similarly, great apologists, philosophers, and theologians from C. S. Lewis and Augustine to Plato and Marcus Aurelius have used metaphor to great effect.

How can you use metaphor? As with similes, look for places in which you can properly leverage an image, and think hard about another person, idea, or thing that resembles the subject you are trying to illuminate. Be fair. Nothing falls flatter than a stale metaphor; but where a statement lacks impact, enliven it with the images conjured by metaphor, and allow the minds of your audience to fill in the gaps. This will both sharpen their grasp of the topic at hand and turn them from recipients of a conversation to participants in it.

---

[5]From Emily Dickinson's *Complete Poems*; http://www.bartleby.com/113/1032.html.

NARRATIVE: PARABLES AND OTHER STORYTELLING TECHNIQUES

It was important for Christ to illuminate his speech with the persuasive power of imagery, but he also had to pull these images into more complex narratives that would stick with his followers and communicate his lessons to them. In a broad sense, Jesus used narrative in three primary ways—to communicate moral lessons through parables and allegories, to cement his teachings and his presence in the broader Jewish (and human) narrative, and to generate a personal narrative that was compelling to his followers and future generations. These narrative forms are intertwined with each other and with the Aristotelian concepts of pathos, logos, and ethos; and they have a remarkable relevance to modern communicators.

Parable and Allegory

Of all Jesus' teaching, the most memorable are his short stories, often referred to as parables. While we are prone to forget the complex admonitions of philosophers, the lessons of Jesus are memorable because they were communicated in a compact narrative form. Tales like the Good Samaritan, the Prodigal Son, and the Pearl of Great Price communicate complex religious, personal, and philosophic lessons as memorable anecdotes that anchor themselves in a listener's memory and allow him to meditate on them long after the story is told. These narratives were made more captivating and colorful through the use of imagery and were told in simple terms appropriate to the historical context of Christ's listeners so that everyone—from prostitutes to tax collectors—could grasp their meaning.

While these stories are often referred to broadly as parables, they are actually a combination of parables and allegories. In his book *Hermeneutics*,[6] Henry A. Virkler claims that a parable can be understood as an extended simile (a comparison of one or two simple, explicit traits using "like" or "as"), while an allegory is an

[6]Henry A. Virkler, *Hermeneutics: Principles and Processes of Biblical Interpretation* (Grand Rapids, MI: Baker Books, 2006), 159.

extended metaphor. Others view parables as compact stories, while allegories are extended, complex narratives with multiple characters and messages. For our purposes, it is most useful to simply refer to Jesus' stories as parables and emphasize a few of their common characteristics. Some of those characteristics are what we call the five C's:

> *Compelling characters:* Jesus' parables almost always contain people (though they occasionally use symbols that stand for people, as in the grain of wheat in John 12:24–26). This serves to put a face on his moral lessons and to add more impactful imagery to his narrative. By discussing his moral lessons through the actions of characters relatable to his listeners, he was able to connect with them more effectively. He used both detail and dialogue to spice up the story.[7]
>
> *Consistent symbolism:* The basic structure of most of Jesus' parables is that one of his characters represents God, and the other characters represent his listeners or the people around them. For instance, in the Parable of the Prodigal Son (discussed at length in Chapter 7 ["Case Studies"] in this book), the father in the story stands for God, while listeners are expected to identify either with the prodigal son or his brother. This is a fairly consistent, clear pattern within Christ's parables. When Jesus strays from this basic structure, he often highlights it clearly.
>
> *Cautious ambiguity:* Jesus rarely gives away the entire point of a story. Rather, he leaves it to the listener to bring his own experiences and draw his own conclusions. As with enthymemes, the power of the parable comes in the reader's participation in the narrative by filling in the gaps.
>
> *Concrete lessons:* The parables always contain one or more moral lessons. In its simplest form, a parable may teach one key concept. In the Parable of the Unjust Judge, for example, Jesus teaches persistence in prayer. In a more complex form (for example, the Good Samaritan or the Prodigal Son) parables teach multiple lessons on multiple levels. The effect depends on the openness of the listener's heart, the focus she affords the story, and the depth of her historical understanding.
>
> *Context:* Jesus had the difficult task of communicating not only to his local community but to the billions of subsequent individuals who

[7]As noted by Kevin Miller in his "3D" system of storytelling. For a fuller treatment of dialogue and detail, see Kevin Miller's "3-D Storytelling," www.preachingtodaysermons.com/3dstorytelling.html.

> would read his words in the New Testament. However, he was always careful to use stories appropriate to the historical and social context of the people to whom he was speaking. To reach the common, oppressed people of first-century Judea, Jesus needed to use characters familiar to his audience—prostitutes, tax collectors, kings, servants, fishermen. Likewise, if you want to reach an audience at a twenty-first-century-real estate convention, it may be inappropriate to lead with a parable about first-century lawyers. Put simply: know your audience.

There are other elements to proper storytelling, but the five C's are what we believe to be the essential components of Christ's parables and can be used by anyone seeking to employ narrative to improve his or her speeches and written communications.

Let's take a closer look at how these elements were used in Jesus' communications by examining the Parable of the Great Supper (Matthew 22:2–14):

> "The kingdom of heaven may be compared to a king who gave a wedding feast for his son, and sent his servants to call those who were invited to the wedding feast, but they would not come. Again he sent other servants, saying, 'Tell those who are invited, See, I have prepared my dinner, my oxen and my fat calves have been slaughtered, and everything is ready. Come to the wedding feast.' But they paid no attention and went off, one to his farm, another to his business, while the rest seized his servants, treated them shamefully, and killed them.
>
> "The king was angry, and he sent his troops and destroyed those murderers and burned their city. Then he said to his servants, 'The wedding feast is ready, but those invited were not worthy. Go therefore to the main roads and invite to the wedding feast as many as you find.' And those servants went out into the roads and gathered all whom they found, both bad and good. So the wedding hall was filled with guests.
>
> "But when the king came in to look at the guests, he saw there a man who had no wedding garment. And he said to him, 'Friend, how did you get in here without a wedding garment?' And he was speechless. Then the king said to the attendants, 'Bind him hand and foot and cast him into the outer darkness. In that place there will be weeping and gnashing of teeth.' For many are called, but few are chosen."

We should immediately notice five elements in this story. First, the characters are clear and compelling. Everyone in Jesus' audience was intimately familiar with the character of a king, and even more familiar with the commoners and the elites. Additionally, the people in his audience were familiar with the king's predicament—a father planning a wedding—which made it easy for them to connect with the story.

Second, for those who followed the pattern of Jesus' communications, the symbolism is clear. The king is God, who is often portrayed in the parables as a king or father or some other person in a position of authority. The elites invited to the wedding most closely align with the religious elites—the Pharisees—in Jewish culture, and the commoners who eventually benefit from the feast are everyday people (like most of those in Christ's audience). The feast itself is the Kingdom of heaven, and the servants are servants of God.

Third, despite the relative clarity of this symbolism, there is a degree of open-endedness in the parable. Jesus doesn't spell out the identity of each character but rather leaves the identification of both the inherent lesson and the symbolism for his listeners to put together. This serves a dual purpose. It causes the listeners to become more involved in the parable, making it more memorable and compelling, and allows them to bring their own experience to the parable, to see it through the lens of their individual lives, enabling them to connect with it more closely.

Theologian Belden Lane explains this concept brilliantly in his article, "Language, Metaphor, and Pastoral Theology":

> As people listened to the stories of Jesus, they never knew *exactly* what he meant. In fact, he was reluctant to speak with a clarity that might forestall the listener's thought and participation. Only with chagrin did he occasionally explain the parables to his disciples (Mk. 4:13; 7:17–18). According to his usage, a parable or metaphor wasn't so much a noun as a verb. It wasn't something he threw out in the form of a complete, finished idea (something to be swallowed like a pill), but it was a *process* that caught people up in its mystery. So we can speak about the experience, not simply of

> listening to parables, but of *being parabled*—of being seized and twisted into new form by its very incompleteness.[8]

Fourth, while Jesus is cautiously ambiguous, the lesson is straightforward for most who take the time to ponder the parable's meaning: the kingdom of heaven is a free gift offered to everyone, but those invited must choose to attend and clothe themselves properly. In the words of Romans 13:14, "But put on the Lord Jesus Christ, and make no provision for the flesh, to gratify its desires." On a deeper level, history enlightens us to the rest of the parable. The servants of the king are like ministers who take the good news of Christ (the invitation to the feast) to the world and are persecuted, rejected, and even killed for their efforts.

Fifth, Jesus uses context as a framing device. He takes the ceremonies and conventions of the time and phrases the parable in a way his listeners would immediately understand. As an added bonus, Christ, the master storyteller, also manages to phrase the parable in such a way that its context is just as relevant two millennia later.

By incorporating these five elements, Christ was able to use the parable to communicate the complex concept of salvation as a gift, with all its accompanying parts (the clothing of Christ, the message of God's ministers, the wide availability of salvation), in a memorable fashion.

Who are the great communicators that you know or recognize? Do they use parables? Many modern ministers like North Point's Andy Stanley and Saddleback's Rick Warren are fond of parables and allegories. Stanley's book on communication, *Communicating for a Change*, even makes use of an extended parable. Pastor and author Max Lucado has made a name for himself as a master storyteller. In the business world, Robert Kiyosaki crafted a very popular modern allegory with his famed book *Rich Dad, Poor Dad*. And in the area of self-help, Robin Sharma wrote an effective parable in his *The Monk Who Sold His Ferrari*.

---

[8] "Language, Metaphor, and Pastoral Theology," *Theology Today*, January 1987, Vol. 43, No. 4, 487.

Like these authors and pastors, you use short stories every day, real and fabricated, to communicate lessons to your children and friends. You just don't think about it. You tell your kids stories from your youth to warn against the dangers of excessive candy consumption and unsafe driving. You repeat fables and fairy tales to warn your students about bad behavior. You even use tales from your past business experiences to communicate lessons to your colleagues at work. These are excellent ways to employ narrative structure, and while Jesus' parables were primarily fiction, you can also use short stories from real life to bring added impact to your communication.

Narrative can also be used as an attention-getter that sets up a longer speech or piece of writing. In his acclaimed work *The Tipping Point*, Malcolm Gladwell uses a story about Hush Puppy shoes to illustrate the importance of word-of-mouth communication and the existence of a "tipping point" at which a product or idea moves from being a niche to a mainstream phenomenon. Good writers often lead with compelling stories that use pathos to lock in readers, involve real or imagined people, and lay out a simple, memorable lesson to carry through to the end of the essay.

Employ narrative within a longer piece of communication to demonstrate a point. Make the stories humorous or serious, real or imagined; but make them memorable, and people will take those points with them. Overall, the key is to review every speech or article you write and ask, is there room for a face? There usually is.

Historical Narrative

When Martin Luther King quoted Scripture, he was doing more than appealing to the Almighty for assistance in the struggle for civil rights—he was placing his peers in a historical narrative, extending their struggle so it melded with the struggle of the biblical people in whom they trusted and from whom they derived their faith. Early spirituals also connected the plight of black Americans to the Israelites in Egypt. For example, consider the song "Marching 'Round Selma":

Marching 'round Selma like Jericho,
Jericho, Jericho
Marching 'round Selma like Jericho
For segregation wall must fall
Look at people answering
To the Freedom Fighters call
Black, Brown and White American say
Segregation must fall
Good evening freedom's fighters
Tell me where you're bound
Tell me where you're marching
"From Selma to Montgomery town"[9]

As noted in the chapter on pathos, these shared artifacts impact people emotionally, and they do so, at least partially, by placing them in the midst of an ongoing historical narrative. These types of communications work by taking an exciting or motivational story from history and placing either the speaker or his audience in the story.

Readers of the Gospels often overlook the fact that Jesus took great pains to fit his ministry into the historical context of Judaism and human history. From the initial proclamations of John the Baptist to Jesus' death on the cross, Jesus' life was a continuance of the Jewish messiah narrative, and his words and actions placed him and his followers firmly within that tradition.

In John 8:58 Jesus makes one of the more shocking statements in the Bible: "Before Abraham was, I am." In one sentence Jesus connects himself with the Jewish story—the story of Abraham—and claims divinity by using the same terminology as God did when he communicated with Abraham. (Earlier Jehovah had answered, "I AM" when Moses asked for his name; Exodus 3:14.)

Other examples abound. In Matthew 5:17–20 Jesus states:

> "Do not think that I have come to abolish the Law or the Prophets; I have not come to abolish them but to fulfill them. For truly, I say to you, until heaven and earth pass away, not an iota, not a dot, will pass from the Law until all is accomplished. Therefore whoever relaxes one of the least of these commandments and teaches others to do the same will be called least in the kingdom of heaven,

[9]"Marching 'Round Selma"; www.negrospirituals.com.

> but whoever does them and teaches them will be called great in the kingdom of heaven. For I tell you, unless your righteousness exceeds that of the scribes and Pharisees, you will never enter the kingdom of heaven."

Simultaneously Jesus cements himself in the tradition of the Law and the Prophets and notes that he is the fulfillment of that story—the climax of Jewish history! While these claims were controversial (indeed, they led to Christ's execution), they grabbed the attention of listeners and placed Christ firmly within the biblical narrative alongside other characters such as Moses and Abraham.

We see modern communicators act out this principle regularly. New CEOs quote old CEOs. Politicians invite comparisons with popular politicians from the past, and modern musicians often link themselves to their idols. Steve Jobs, one of the most adept storytellers in all of corporate America, continually evolves the story of Apple as a tale of technological tipping points from the PC to the first effective MP3 player. Employees at companies such as GE, McKinsey, and Coca-Cola often take pride in being a part of the storied traditions of their companies. Similarly, all of us tell family stories at reunions to keep the narratives alive and extend them from generation to generation. This type of historical narrative links your audience to a cause larger than themselves and places them firmly within a respected tradition.

Where can you incorporate historical narrative in your communications? If you are speaking at a college commencement, is it possible to link your audience to the noble deeds of the college's founder? If you are giving a business presentation, can you place the current problem within the historical context of the industry or company and generate a sense of pride and ownership among the other employees? If you coach a basketball team, how can you use narrative to make your current team feel part of a long and successful tradition?

Incorporating historical narrative into your communications can be as simple as knowing your context and the history of that context and then incorporating that history into your communications. By linking history to the present, you can conjure the power of the past.

Personal Narrative

Acclaimed Victorian playwright Oscar Wilde was as famous for his public life as for the quality of his written works. Personally and professionally he was a proponent of aestheticism—a movement that championed superficiality in literature, the supremacy of beauty or art for art's sake. They claimed art need not convey a message but simply be beautiful. He wrote with lavish humor about the absurdity of Victorian sensibilities and flaunted them at every turn. He wore his hair long, dressed in the style of a "dandy," and hung pictures of sunflowers around his room. He lived the life of a London socialite even when the expenses of such a life were beyond his personal means. In doing so, he became more than a proponent of aestheticism—he became the walking image of aestheticism. As Wilde once observed, "An idea is of no value until it becomes incarnate and is made an image."

While Wilde and Jesus have almost no other parallels, that description is the essence of Christ. In his incarnation, he gave human form to the perfection described and exemplified by God. He was an idea of perfection, an incarnate image.

From a narrative perspective, this is brilliant, and it is closely related to the concept of ethos. God knew that the law as laid out in the Old Testament was confusing and hard to remember; so he sent his Son to earth as a person in whom we could see the perfection of the law. By making the Word flesh, God made Jesus a model for holiness. He communicated the perfection of the law through the person of Jesus Christ.

Obviously you cannot employ personal narrative in quite the same way; but many communicators find strength in the story of their own lives. If you can formulate a coherent story for your life, with a history, a purpose, a character, and a destiny, you can more effectively bring a message aligned with that character and destiny to your readers and listeners. This is more than the development of ethos. This is an incarnation of your ideas. You have to, in a phrase, "eat, sleep, and breathe" them.

That is what Thoreau did on Walden Pond, it's what Solzhenitsyn did in his writings about the gulags, and it is what Nelson Mandela did in both his suffering and forgiveness in South Africa. For you, the power of personal narrative may be as simple as practicing what you preach, and it will make you much more effective as a communicator. For those of us without a 100 percent clear set of life goals or values, ideals or messages, it can be as simple as taking time to think through our values and our direction and committing to more fully live out that ideology. As we do so, we will begin to be able to incorporate that narrative into our communications, simultaneously bringing color to our writing and speech and building the ethos of a consistent character.

CONCEPT REVIEW

Simile: An explicit comparison using "like," "as," or "than."

Metaphor: A direct comparison or equivocation that relies on imagery to create an implicit association.

Parable or allegory: A short story that communicates a moral lesson, composed with attention to the five C's—compelling characters, consistent symbolism, cautious ambiguity, concrete lessons, and context.

Historical narrative: An ongoing, real-world narrative in which a rhetor can place her audience.

Personal narrative: An individual's life story that, as part of his or her rhetoric or the rhetoric of his or her followers, can convey powerful messages.

QUESTIONS FOR FURTHER CONSIDERATION

1. Do you have a favorite parable or allegory? What is it? Why is it memorable?
2. Review your last piece of written communication. Did you employ any imagery or narrative? Are there places in which you might have?
3. Think of a story that confused you. Why was it confusing? Was that confusion bad, or did it lead you to more fully consider the situation?

CHAPTER FIVE

DISCIPLESHIP

SPREADING AND SUSTAINING THE MESSAGE

On May 22, 1787, twelve British men formed a group known as the Committee for the Abolition of the Slave Trade.[1] Today opposition to slavery seems commonsensical. We live in a world in which slavery was officially abolished in the United States nearly 150 years ago and in most of the world by 1926, but for those men in 1787 the cause of abolition was as fanciful as it was unpopular.

Almost every empire in history fostered slavery in some form. As early as 2600 B.C., Egyptian rulers were forcing foreign peoples to erect pyramids, and the early Mesopotamian Code of Hammurabi notes slavery as one of the region's established institutions. The Greeks and Romans, the Indians and the Chinese all viewed slavery as a common practice, often subjugating conquered peoples or inferior domestic classes, sometimes dividing those classes along racial or ethnic lines. And while we think of slavery as a violation of basic human rights, even world religions failed to take a clear stand condemning the institution.

So it was truly revolutionary for twelve men in Britain to step forward at the height of the Atlantic slave trade and openly state their dedication to eradicating the institution. In fact, the only thing more preposterous than their attempt to abolish slavery in Britain (and subsequently the world) was the speed with which they achieved their goal.

The Committee, comprised of nine Quakers and three evan-

[1]John Coffey, "The Abolition of the Slave Trade: Christian Conscience and Political Action," *Cambridge Papers*, June 2006, Vol. 15, No. 2.

gelical Christians (Thomas Clarkson, William Wilberforce, and Granville Sharpe), found in abolitionism a truly Christian cause. In France the cause of abolition had remained small, a pet cause of the liberal elite. But in Britain the Committee for the Abolition of the Slave Trade, the Quakers, and other groups were about to make it a grassroots campaign.[2]

From a core of twelve men (echoing the twelve disciples) rose a popular movement millions strong. Employing artists, writers, politicians, and housewives, the Committee and its sympathizers created visual arts, pamphlets, and books to hammer home the horrors of slavery. Thomas Clarkson traveled more than thirty thousand miles around Great Britain organizing lectures and assembling and spreading information.[3] Most importantly, these men worked tirelessly to create disciples at home and abroad. In pockets around the U.K. women held antislavery meetings in their parlors. In the U.S. homegrown abolitionists and disciples of their forebears in Great Britain organized strong popular uprisings against the peculiar institution and also practical acts of rebellion such as the Underground Railroad. Masses of individuals, usually organized in small, dispersed clusters, distributed literature, engaged in debates, hosted political rallies, and cultivated the relationships necessary to convert others to the cause.

The efforts of these small groups proved to be remarkably successful. By the mid-1800s Britain abolished a 5,000-year-old institution, and in less than a hundred years those small clusters of Christian men and women had fanned a small flame of hope into the roaring fire of nineteenth-century abolitionism, changing the world forever.

That is the power of discipleship.

The *Random House Unabridged Dictionary* defines a disciple as "a person who is a pupil or an adherent of the doctrines of another." Whether in multi-level marketing businesses like Amway,

[2]"Committee for the Abolition of the Slave Trade," http://en.wikipedia.org/wiki/Committee_for_the_Abolition_of_the_Slave_Trade (accessed November 17, 2007).
[3]See http://new.edp24.co.uk/content/PlaceinHistory/content/37Clarkson.aspx; also, unofficial notes taken from Stephen Davies's lecture at the Institute for Humane Studies, Advanced Studies in Freedom conference, July 7–13, 2007 at Loyola University (Chicago).

office mentorship programs, or historical movements, you've likely encountered the concept of discipleship and the power it has when combined with the dual concepts of cellular networks and small groups. In Christianity, discipleship is the process of transforming a person from being the recipient of a message to an active participant in that message. Discipleship was the key way in which Jesus Christ and his followers transmitted the message of Christianity to "the ends of the earth" (Acts 13:47).

So how did Jesus do it? Modern organization gurus are just catching on to the power of cellular organizations. But two thousand years ago Jesus and his followers organized the Christian church as a distinctively cellular and discipleship-oriented institution. This structure allowed the new religion to quickly spread from a forgotten corner of the Roman Empire to the heights of global power. And that movement and the forms that catalyzed it show both the remarkable power of Christian discipleship and the ways in which that form of organization can be relevant to many spheres of organization and communication today.

The discipleship model is a rigorous, relationship-oriented, and complex system of message communication and replication that requires a great deal of time and energy. Not everything you do necessitates the formation of such a complex web of organization. However, for those critical messages—whether you're managing a political campaign, spreading the gospel, or attempting to spearhead a strategic turnaround in your small business—the lessons of discipleship can be essential to your success. Here's how Jesus did it—and how you can follow his example.

BUILD THE CORE

Just as every great structure needs a solid foundation, every movement requires a small core of devoted individuals. Discipleship starts with the small group.

As Christ approached the task of sending his message of hope and salvation from Jerusalem to the rest of the world, his first priority was to create a few small, solid groups of individuals totally dedicated to the message who could sustain it in his absence. This task was essential to his ministry. Indeed, one of Christ's first substantial acts as he began to preach was to gather disciples.

According to the first chapter of John, the day after he was baptized, even before his first miracle, Jesus began to call disciples. His immediate priority was gathering devoted followers around him, teaching them, and developing close relationships with them as he spread his message.

Readers of the Gospels are familiar with Christ's closest allies. The core consisted of the twelve apostles who traveled with him until the time of his arrest. That group might also be expanded, though, to include a few other essential figures including Jesus' mother, Mary Magdalene, and John the Baptist (who was, in a way, discipled by the Father). But beyond that small cadre of close friends, Jesus also assembled another, larger group of disciples to supplement that foundational core. Luke 10:1 notes that Jesus gathered together seventy-two disciples after sending forth his twelve apostles and "sent them on ahead of him, two by two, into every town and place where he himself was about to go." Various other medium-sized groups of close followers are described or alluded to in passages such as the Sermon on the Mount. However you classify his disciples, what is clear is that while Jesus taught thousands of people around the countryside and healed multitudes in the course of his three-year travels, he cultivated closer relationships with at least two smaller groups, one of which numbered only twelve people. He taught them the most important lessons. He allowed them the privilege of witnessing every moment of his ministry firsthand. And he entrusted them with bearing witness to the things they had seen.

Jesus also assured that these small groups of men and women were absolutely committed to his message. Christ was very clear that serving as one of his disciples would be a taxing experience:

> As they were going along the road, someone said to him, "I will follow you wherever you go."
>
> And Jesus said to him, "Foxes have holes, and birds of the air have nests, but the Son of Man has nowhere to lay his head."

> To another he said, "Follow me." But he said, "Lord, let me first go and bury my father." And Jesus said to him, "Leave the dead to bury their own dead. But as for you, go and proclaim the kingdom of God."
>
> Yet another said, "I will follow you, Lord, but let me first say farewell to those at my home." Jesus said to him, "No one who puts his hand to the plow and looks back is fit for the kingdom of God." (Luke 9:57–62)

Jesus was unambiguous about what was expected of his followers. To be one of his disciples—to be included in the inner circle—one had to be ready for exceptional dedication and sacrifice. Jesus knew that to maintain an effective core he needed people who were committed to bearing witness above all else and who realized that only sacrifice and selflessness could create the type of foundation he needed to reach the world. In return for such devotion, Jesus stood up for them, empowered them, trusted them, cried in front of them, answered their sincere questions, and forgave them when they strayed. He built a relationship of mutual trust and support, even asking them to keep watch while he prayed. By committing himself fully to those in his core group, he solidified their loyalty to him.

Similar models of core building can be found in business, politics, and sports. CEOs have close-knit groups of intelligent, hard-nosed people who surround them at the top of corporate pyramids and generate critical leadership within the larger company. Great leaders such as John F. Kennedy and Napoleon Bonaparte surround themselves with trusted advisers who believe wholly in the common cause of the group and are trained to advance it. Sprawling online communities like Daily Kos are sustained by a critical few who fight fiercely to spread key messages to the larger group. Great academics such as Socrates, Freud, and Pythagoras assembled small groups of devoted followers who replicated their teachings. Even athletes are at their greatest when they, like Michael Jordan throughout the 1980s and 1990s, are surrounded by teammates dedicated to building a cohesive and mutually supportive group.

Where do you need to build a core? Which messages, movements, and organizations might require you to assemble a core team of disciples? The obvious answer is that you need a core group of family and friends dedicated to support mutual development and spiritual growth.

Beyond this, whether you are attempting to set the strategy of a sales team or leading a grassroots effort to lobby Congress, you'll need disciples. You will need to assure their dedication to the cause (with the level of dedication determined by the seriousness of the cause—rarely will you need to lead a movement that justifies followers' abandoning their families!). And you will need to build a core of people who in turn have their own independent cores to advance the message beyond your limited sphere of influence.

When building your core, pick people who are loyal but willing to challenge you. Select those who are willing to sacrifice. Spend time with them, cultivating close personal bonds that will sustain the group through difficult times. Invest—teaching them and listening to them—and open your heart to them. No core is stable without some measure of personal or professional trust. Let people invest in you just as much as you invest in them.

WORK IN CELLS AND SMALL GROUPS

Once this core is established, it must be transformed into a cellular or small-group-based organization. As we've noted, Jesus' formation of a core group of disciples was effective because it was small, relationship-oriented, personal in nature, and required mutual sacrifice. However, as organizations and movements grow, a contradiction arises. You want new people to hear your message and join in the cause, but it is more difficult to create relationships with all these new people and get real dedication from them. The original leader simply doesn't have the time or resources to mentor everyone, and the close cohesion of the group suffers as a result of growth.

Writer Malcolm Gladwell described this process in a *New Yorker* article on Rick Warren's success at Saddleback Church:

> Churches, like any large voluntary organization, have at their core a contradiction. In order to attract newcomers, they must have low barriers to entry. They must be unintimidating, friendly, and

> compatible with the culture they are a part of. In order to retain their membership, however, they need to have an identity distinct from that culture. They need to give their followers a sense of community—and community, exclusivity, a distinct identity are all, inevitably, casualties of growth. As an economist would say, the bigger an organization becomes, the greater a freerider problem it has. If I go to a church with five hundred members, in a magnificent cathedral, with spectacular services and music, why should I volunteer or donate any substantial share of my money? What kind of peer pressure is there in a congregation that large? If the barriers to entry become too low—and the ties among members become increasingly tenuous—then a church as it grows bigger becomes weaker.[4]

This is a common problem with growing organizations. People can be initially moved by a message, but they need to be part of a community that reinforces that message interpersonally to maintain their dedication. As churches, corporations, or government entities increase in size, people grow less connected, and each individual's dedication to the cause and to the group decreases. The movement itself grows less effective.

So how do you adjust for these growing pains? Gladwell continues:

> One solution to the problem is simply not to grow, and, historically, churches have sacrificed size for community. But there is another approach: to create a church out of a network of lots of little church cells—exclusive, tightly knit groups of six or seven who meet in one another's homes during the week to worship and pray. The small group as an instrument of community is initially how Communism spread, and in the postwar years Alcoholics Anonymous and its twelve-step progeny perfected the small-group technique. . . . When churches—in particular, the megachurches that became the engine of the evangelical movement, in the nineteen-seventies and eighties—began to adopt the cellular model, they found out the same thing. The small group was an extraordinary vehicle of commitment. It was personal and flexible. It cost nothing. It was convenient, and every worshipper was able to find a small group that precisely matched his or her interests. Today,

[4]Malcolm Gladwell, "The Cellular Church," *The New Yorker*, September 12, 2005.

> at least forty million Americans are in a religiously based small group, and the growing ranks of small-group membership have caused a profound shift in the nature of the American religious experience.[5]

This personal, flexible nature is one of the reasons the discipleship method modeled by Christ is so compelling. Jesus not only delivered a brilliant message and gathered around him a core group of believers, he also modeled the organization necessary to sustain and grow that message while maintaining its impact and intimacy. During his earthly ministry Christ created a small core of people that he sent out to gather other small groups. In turn these groups gathered their own groups. Before long there were small cellular organizations—churches—spread throughout the Middle East. Just as Christ sent forward pairs of disciples to prepare his way in Luke 10, he sent his disciples themselves out after his death to train new leaders, adapt to local customs, and create compelling cellular organizations in new regions with new people. The apostle Paul was indisputably Jesus' most brilliant student in disciple-making. Paul not only gathered key leaders around him and trained them but mentored the churches they formed through his letters and lecture tours.

Cellular, small-group-oriented organizations continue to enjoy immense success. Those who study organization now note the importance of small, intimate groups like the twelve disciples and put the maximum number of personal connections one can have at somewhere around one hundred and fifty (larger than the second group of disciples mentored by Christ).[6] Numerous modern organizations adhere to these principles in order to exploit the flexibility, adaptability, dedication, and mutual trust they foster. As mentioned, Alcoholics Anonymous uses small groups to promote accountability and foster intimacy. Harvard Business School breaks its large, nine-hundred-person class into multiple sections of around ninety students, and these sections are further complemented by study

[5]Ibid.

[6]Malcolm Gladwell, *The Tipping Point—How Little Things Make a Big Difference* (Boston: Little, Brown and Company, 2000).

groups of six students. Military organizations have long realized that soldiers cannot be dedicated to the entire army in the same way they can be dedicated to small units; fraternities and sororities gain incredible dedication from their members by personalizing the college experience; and the house church movement has been successful worldwide because it relies on closely knit groups that foster peer pressure, accountability, and trust.

The same dynamic can be seen in families. Extended families tend to work best when they are loosely bound by the leaders of each cellular unit. Have you ever been to a family reunion? There is usually a matriarch or patriarch (typically one of the oldest family members) with strong ties to the next generation (your parents or grandparents). Each person in that subsequent generation maintains a smaller functioning extended family of aunts, uncles, and cousins, and you in turn have your own spouse and children that you link to the larger body. All of these family units are distinct and have a unique personality, but they are bound loosely to the larger unit by the successful discipleship of the previous generation.

Cellular organizations and small groups are similarly essential to you as you attempt to communicate your messages and build support. When you see your organization or movement growing, do not make the trade-off between size and substance. Try to find ways to create smaller, individualized communities that can nurture themselves and the larger group. The tools at your disposal are numerous. Small groups function best in person, but you can also link those groups with online discussion forums, newsletters, conference calls (in the case of businesses), blogs, and strategically planned retreats (or, as your family might call them, vacations). Never let people fall out of these groups. Get everyone involved, and when individual units get too large, break them into smaller units that can better foster intimacy and trust.

TRAIN THE TRAINERS

We know that small groups are more effective and that cellular organizations foster better relationships and increased dedication. But how do you establish and manage a widely dispersed network of tens, hundreds, or thousands of loosely bound groups? The answer, once again, lies in combining the discipleship model with a model of cellular organization. Great leaders don't simply train followers; they train other leaders, who in turn train other leaders, and the networks of dedicated people fan out around them in concentric circles. In the business jargon this is referred to as the train-the-trainer approach.

Train-the-trainer is readily evident in the example we used at the introduction of this chapter. The abolitionist movement in England was not simply a movement of twelve men and millions of followers. It was the story of small groups of men and women who convinced others to take a leadership role in the cause, thereby spreading both the message of abolitionism and the organizational model to extend and sustain that message. These leaders mentored one another, and their circles of influence extended throughout Britain and then overseas to all the colonies and former colonies of the British Empire.

Similarly, the train-the-trainer approach was modeled by the early Christian church as it followed the example of Christ. Jesus didn't merely train Peter and John to be dedicated servants. He trained them to reach other people and make them disciples, assuring that the system he set up would self-replicate to the millions who would eventually be impacted by the small groups these original disciples formed. Jesus didn't just teach his disciples to lead good lives; he taught them to teach others to lead good lives. Following Christ meant replicating all his actions, including his model of leadership.

This is likely one of the reasons that Jesus took his disciples with him to watch him preach. That was a form of apprenticeship. As he spoke to crowds, the select few who traveled with him not only learned the principles about which he spoke, but the methods Jesus used to deliver them. His example was replicated as the original disciples went forth after his resurrection. Similarly, in Paul's letters to Timothy we find that Paul mentored Timothy not only in the content of Christianity but in its transmission to others. Many of the disciples traveled at least part of the time with other younger or less experienced disciples they were training to take their places. In Acts

4 Peter and John traveled together, mentoring and supporting one another. Likewise, Paul himself was mentored and apprenticed by Barnabas. When Paul and Barnabas took separate routes to Antioch to revisit all of the churches they had raised on previous journeys in Acts 15:36–41, each took another disciple with him. Much of the book of the Acts of the Apostles is the story of leaders in training.

The most effective modern churches follow this example. Even as the influence of hierarchical religious organizations has faded in Western Europe, the evangelical church and associated cellular religious organizations such as the Mormon Church are spreading rapidly in places like Africa and the United States. As mentioned before, Rick Warren's Saddleback Church is growing quickly because it utilizes a train-the-trainer approach. Warren himself lectures extensively at churches around the world for the purpose of training other church leaders to replicate his cellular church success. In Atlanta, Andy Stanley's North Point Church has set a goal of one hundred thousand people in small groups in the Atlanta area. Stanley has trained leaders of several other churches, including Buckhead Church and Browns Bridge Community Church, to take the same model into the broader community. Stanley in turn was influenced by Charles Stanley, Chicago's Willow Creek Community Church, and countless other individuals and organizations. Throughout the United States, many of the fastest-growing churches are those that are led by people mentored by other leaders and taught to self-replicate, generating a new generation of leaders (not just followers) much like themselves.

Successful corporations do the same. Many large organizations offer management training programs and rigorous mentorship programs to assure that leaders, not just followers, emerge. McKinsey & Company relies on the fact that all of its consultants are leaders, mentored by more senior consultants and by peers who are capable of enabling others to lead within their client organizations. The success of the firm is indicated not just by its reputation in the business community but by the leaders they cultivate internally and in the organizations with which they work. Other companies, like Toyota, look to encourage problem-solving leadership even among junior personnel. Amway is built on the principle that senior salespeople can train others to do exactly what they do (including training even more people to follow in their footsteps). Across the spectrum, companies are realizing that the increasing necessity of small groups and adaptability in the workforce requires discipleship by people who are willing to train others to be leaders like themselves.

When you communicate, are you training leaders or followers? In your family, do you teach your sons and daughters to be excellent parents or merely excellent sons and daughters? At work, are you taking the time to mentor others—to train them to train others—or are you just punching a time card and demanding results from those in your employ? It is not enough to teach people the skills to do *their* jobs. You must teach them the skills to do *your* job, and in that way they can expand the organization and spread the message through effective discipleship.

GENERATE SUPPORTING MATERIAL

Subsequently, the leaders you train must be equipped with the materials and tools they need to spread a message and maintain focus. Without firm supporting materials, messages become diluted. People make them too adaptable, taking them in their own directions, and the coherence of the message disappears. But with the appropriate supporting tools and materials, messages and organizations can stay focused even as they expand.

In Jesus' three-year ministry, it appears that his attempt to give his followers the materials to replicate his message was confined to oral transmission, primarily in the form of preaching and private instruction. In our media-centric age, such an approach may be too simplistic to be effective. Granted, Jesus was a rhetorical genius (as we've detailed in the preceding chapters) who utilized logos, pathos, and ethos and wielded narrative and imagery to hammer those messages home. But he was not multimedia. He did not paint or write. He had no computers to work with and no Internet on which to blog or hold group chats. In the broader context of Christian communication, however, Christ laid the foundation for the creation of these materials and, at least as Christians understand it, directly inspired others to generate supporting materials for him.

First among these supporting materials is the Bible. In his second epistle to Timothy, Paul wrote, "All Scripture is breathed out by God and profitable for teaching, for reproof, for correction, and for training in righteousness" (3:16). It is clear from both the Old and New Testaments that God considered the Bible his leadership and followership training manual. It was designed as an authoritative source for proper Christian training, influenced by the hand of God himself. Writers such as Paul recorded these materials on behalf of God, but they are the materials Christ intended to leave behind to guide the church he had created.

Second, the writings of Christian leaders extend beyond the Old and New Testament canons to various other epistles, gospels, and philosophic works. Writers such as St. Augustine, C. S. Lewis, and Thomas Aquinas took it upon themselves to add to the materials Christians could use in sorting out their world and their beliefs. Many modern writers such as Francis Schaeffer, John Piper, R. C. Sproul, Charles Stanley, Max Lucado, and Pope John Paul II have perpetuated this tradition, disseminating everything from philosophy to poetry throughout the world. Of course, these are secondary texts that do not hold the authority of the Bible itself. They are merely useful tools for Christians approaching their commission to witness to the world, but they are supporting materials.

Beyond the written word, great Christian artists (such as Rembrandt), musicians (such as Johann Sebastian Bach), and bloggers (such as Biola University professors Fred Sanders and John Mark Reynolds) have used visual media and new media to create ever-evolving tools for modern Christians to understand the heart of God and spread his message. And the overall basket of supporting materials for the Christian faith is comprehensive.

Other great thinkers and leaders mirror this example. At the time of the Revolutionary War in the United States, Thomas Paine released pamphlets such as *Common Sense*; and in the aftermath of the war, thinkers such as James Madison used newspapers, lectures, and pamphlets to argue for a federalist system of government. When a politician like Hillary Clinton runs for office, she doesn't just travel the lecture circuit. She sets up websites, generates newsletters and policy briefings, creates MySpace and Facebook accounts, and authorizes autobiographies from sympathetic devotees. These people realize the importance of supporting materials in discipleship—just as Christ realized the importance of Scripture in the focused spread of the early Christian church—and seek new ways to innovate with the media at their disposal.

Likewise, businesses issue annual reports and company newsletters and set up complex public relations departments. Internal knowledge-sharing network companies now reach the public in numerous ways, and these tools have allowed corporations to grow ever larger in a decentralized way. Koch Industries owner Charles Koch went so far as to release a book on his management philosophy, *The Science of Success*, and McKinsey & Company regularly publishes short editorials in publications such as *The Economist*, detailed features in *The McKinsey Quarterly* (a magazine), and lengthy books like *Valuation* to forward vital messages.

As a modern communicator, you have unprecedented modes of content delivery at your disposal. You can utilize user-generated wikis to create both a sense of community and up-to-date information about your project. You can use group blogs to release new information to constituents and maintain personal interactions without face-to-face contact. You can use mass e-mail, hard-copy newsletters, or even self-published books (courtesy of sites such as lulu.com) to communicate firm organizational messages that followers can latch onto and learn from. You can also use podcasts or YouTube videos to put a voice or face with the message you communicate. All these tools are either free or inexpensive. You simply have to determine which ones are best suited to your message and your audience and how you can most effectively employ them.

REACH OUT

Finally, a compelling message, a solid model of discipleship, a network of small groups, and a plethora of supporting materials are worth nothing if you fail to engage in outreach. With respect to the witness of Christianity, Christ referred to this as the Great Commission.

Christ did not come to save the eighty-four people he specifically named as disciples in the Gospels. As John 3:16 famously notes, "For God so loved the world, that he gave his only Son, that whoever believes in him should not perish but have eternal life." Jesus came to save the whole world. And to do that, he needed to reach vast numbers of people—even those who were not inclined to agree with him—and to attempt to persuade them of the truth of sin and the necessity of repentance and salvation. Christ's heart was the heart of a seeker, and his greatest pleasure was not relaxing in the embrace of his admirers, but finding and saving those who did not know or trust him.

According to Jesus, the number one thing that excites the Father is conversion. In Luke 19:10 Jesus states, "For the Son of Man came to seek and to save the lost." And in the Parable of the Lost Sheep Jesus states, "Just so, I tell you, there will be more joy in heaven over one sinner who repents than over ninety-nine righteous persons who need no repentance" (Luke 15:7). Jesus regularly spent time not with the religious leaders but with prostitutes, criminals, and tax collectors because they were the ones who most desperately needed his message and his help and knew it. And after his resurrection Jesus provided clear instructions for his disciples: "All authority in heaven and on earth has been given to me. Go therefore and make disciples of all nations, baptizing them in the name of the Father and of the Son and of the Holy Spirit, teaching them to observe all that I have commanded you" (Matthew 28:18–20).

Christ knew that he was training his disciples to reach new groups, to expand the number of cells in the church, and to grow the community of those who believed. This was never going to be an easy assignment. Jesus and many of his followers died for the message, winning hearts and making enemies as they preached the gospel. But they knew you cannot spread a message by preaching to the choir; you cannot grow an organization without seeking converts.

So Christ commanded his disciples not only to stick together but to disperse. While they were expected to mentor and support one another, the heart of the Great Commission required that they spread out in order to transmit the message of Jesus. It was necessary for his followers to set out into uncharted territories and address those who had never been exposed to Christ's words. Jesus told the disciples they were "the salt of the earth . . . the light of the world" (Matthew 5:13–14). Jesus knew that salt was a preservative in the ancient world, that a little bit of salt goes a long way toward affecting everything around it. He also knew that light is stronger than darkness, that even a pinprick of light in a sea of darkness can illuminate its environment and give hope to onlookers. So rather than encouraging his followers to seek comfort with one another all the time (they certainly did some of the time), he encouraged them to be adventurous and to set out to impact the world.

Spreading important messages is hard work. When Thomas Clarkson set out riding around the English countryside to fight the evil of slavery, he faced hostile audiences and violent slave owners. But it was by seeking new followers that he spread a lifesaving message from a small group of twelve to the entire western world. He was salt; he was light. A core believer in abolitionism, trained to be a leader reinforced by a small community of like-minded people, and equipped with the skills and facts to combat the peculiar institution of slavery, he went out into the world and reached out to those who did not believe.

Martin Luther King Jr. did the same, making common cause with whites in America at a time when many African-Americans chose (perhaps justifiably) to vilify them. Thomas Jefferson did this when he wrote the Declaration of Independence, proclaiming the grievances of the colonies publicly to the entire world. Glaceau CEO J. Darius Bikoff did this, selling his bottles of enriched water from the back of his car. It is easy to get complacent when you do not have to face the hostility and loneliness of reaching out to the unconverted. It is even easier to lose touch with the world around you when you are surrounded by an echo chamber of like-minded people who never challenge your views. But it is by reaching out to others and taking a leap of faith that you ultimately spread a message or grow an organization.

This is, of course, particularly critical for the modern church, the most powerful cellular organization in the world. Toward the end of his *New Yorker* piece Malcolm Gladwell includes a lengthy quote by Rick Warren:

> There is only one thing big enough to handle the world's problems, and that is the millions and millions of churches spread out around the world. I can take you to thousands of villages where they don't have a school. They don't have a grocery store, don't have a fire department. But they have a church. They have a pastor. They have volunteers. The problem today is distribution. In the tsunami, millions of dollars of foodstuffs piled up on the shores and people couldn't get it into the places that needed it, because they didn't have a network. Well, the biggest distribution network in the world is local churches. There are millions of them, far more than all the franchises in the world. Put together, they could be a force for good.[7]

Warren recognizes that there is power in discipleship and the cellular model, and that power is ours to use for good. It isn't there solely to reach others for Christ, though that is a critical mission. It is there, more broadly, to help people—struggling, fragile people like you and me. It ended slavery. It subverted the cruelties of the Roman Empire. It is fighting poverty and disease in Africa and beyond. And it has the power to be the most revolutionary force on the planet if we choose to use it well.

[7]Gladwell, "The Cellular Church."

CONCEPT REVIEW

Core: A small group of dedicated leaders who serve as the foundation of a movement or an organization.

Discipleship: The act of mentoring followers, based largely on the development of personal relationships; transforming someone from being the recipient of a message to being an active participant in that message.

Cellular organization: A movement or organization composed of small, loosely connected groups that provide a flexible, adaptable model for growth based on community, local knowledge, and discipleship.

Small group: One of the "cells" in an organization; and a limited collection of individuals who share a common goal or set of beliefs that reinforces itself through mutual respect, trust, and discipleship.

Train-the-trainer: The process by which disciples are not merely trained to follow but to lead, replicating the discipleship model with other cells in an organization.

Supporting material: All of the materials, media, and tools used to sustain a message and communicate it to adherents of the message.

Outreach: The process by which individuals in an organization or movement attempt to gain new followers or converts, reaching out to those opposed to or unaware of the organization or message.

QUESTIONS FOR FURTHER CONSIDERATION

1. Do you have mentors? Do you mentor others? In what ways are you training disciples, and in what ways have you been trained?
2. Which organizations have the best models for mentorship or discipleship? Which organizations are worst? What separates the two?
3. Which cellular organizations work best, and which work worst? What separates the two?
4. What is the difference between training leaders and training followers? What makes a good leader? Can you think of someone who has trained you to train others? Describe that experience.
5. Give an example of an organization without outreach. What is the impact of that lack of outreach on growth? What is the impact on members of the existing community?
6. What organization or message with which you are involved could benefit most from the principles outlined in this chapter? What concrete steps can you take to make that happen?

CHAPTER SIX

HEAVENLY HEURISTICS

RHETORIC'S RULES OF THUMB

Most people have never heard of Mary Schmich. Born in Savannah, Georgia, and raised in Arizona, Schmich is an accomplished columnist for the *Chicago Tribune* and is best known for a single column she wrote in June 1997.[1] At that time she published what seemed like a perennial cliché—the commencement address she would have given if asked. It centered around one critical piece of advice: wear sunscreen.

Sound familiar? It should. In 1998 Australian film director Baz Luhrmann set Schmich's column to music, hired voice actor Lee Perry to record it, and released a music single, "Everybody's Free (to Wear Sunscreen)," that went on to top the charts and enjoy play at numerous graduation ceremonies.[2] It is simple and spoken word. Comprised of a series of pithy and humorous admonitions to young people, it is an excellent illustration of common-sense aphorism in the vein of Confucius, Mark Twain, and Yogi Berra. In part it reads:

> *Ladies and Gentlemen of the class of '97*
> *Wear Sunscreen . . .*
> *Enjoy the power and beauty of your youth. Oh, never mind.*
> *you will not understand the power and beauty of your youth until they've faded.*
> *But trust me, in 20 years you'll look back at photos of yourself*
> *and recall in a way you can't grasp now, how much*
> *possibility lay before you*
> *and how fabulous you really looked,*

[1]Mary Schmich, "Advice, Like Youth, Probably Just Wasted on the Young," *Chicago Tribune*, June 1, 1997.
[2]CD information at http://www.discogs.com/viewimages?what=R&obid=476994.

you are not as fat as you imagine.
Don't worry about the future, or worry, but know that worrying is as effective as trying to solve an algebra equation by chewing bubblegum.
The real troubles in your life are apt to be things that never crossed your worried mind, the kind that blindside you at 4 pm on some idle Tuesday.
Do one thing every day that scares you
Sing Don't be reckless with other people's hearts. Don't put up with people who are reckless with yours.
Floss[3]

Rather than delivering a complex logical treatise on the nature of the good life, Schmich dispatches a few actionable rules of thumb. They are not systematic, exhaustive, or properly categorized, but they are helpful nonetheless.

The preceding five chapters of this book have explained several methods by which Jesus communicated with his followers, highlighting in some detail the way other communicators have employed the same techniques and ways you can replicate them.

However, there are a number of "rules of rhetoric" used by Jesus that defy categorization or deserve to be highlighted individually. These are heuristics—the fancy name for "rules of thumb"—that illuminate more fully the character of Christ's communication and can have an enormous impact on the ways in which you communicate with others.

This chapter attempts to capture those heuristics. Every heuristic does not apply in every situation. These are, after all, rules of thumb and not universal truths. But this list contains a decent sampling of actionable aphorisms drawn from the New Testament that can be useful to your everyday communications.

YOUR BASIC MESSAGE SHOULD CONTAIN GOOD NEWS[4]

Almost every message should contain some tidbit of good news. The word *gospel* itself means "good news," and it is a mark of Christ's

[3]Schmich, "Advice, Like Youth, Probably Just Wasted on the Young."
[4]The first three points in this section all relate to points made by Rick Warren in his helpful essay "A Primer on Preaching Like Jesus, Part 1"; http://www.pastors.com/RWMT/?ID=47&artid=1595&expand=1.

communication that he always gave his followers a reason for hope. In his essay, "A Primer on Preaching Like Jesus," Pastor Rick Warren writes of the impact good news can have on people:

> Crowds always flock to Good News. These days, particularly after September 11th, there is plenty of bad news in the world. The last thing people need to hear is more bad news in church. They're looking for hope and help and encouragement. Jesus understood this. That's why he felt so compassionate toward them. He knew that the crowds were "harassed and helpless, like sheep without a shepherd."[5]

In John 3:17 Jesus notes, "For God did not send his Son into the world to condemn the world, but in order that the world might be saved through him." Matthew 11:28 records Jesus' invitation, "Come to me, all who labor and are heavy laden, and I will give you rest." Half of Jesus' message was bad news—our sinfulness and need of salvation. The other half was good news—our way out.

This concept also has broad applicability beyond the Gospels. Whenever you communicate, seek to incorporate some good news. Even if your primary message is bad news, dissatisfaction, or condemnation, offer the audience a reason to hope, a way out of the situation, or a way they can help. Give people a concrete means to act. If you have to criticize people, also mention something they are doing right or give them a way to correct their actions.

START WITH YOUR AUDIENCE'S NEEDS

Why does Jesus repeatedly connect salvation to water for the thirsty and bread for the hungry? Why does he call God the shepherd, and his people sheep? Why is the message of grace so compelling to Jesus' audiences, composed of thoroughly sinful people?

The answer is simple. If you want to persuade people, start with their needs. Some needs are universal. Everyone requires love, friendship, food, water, shelter, and security. Some needs are contingent or relative (poor people need money more than rich people; debtors need debt-relief; the sick need medical care).

---

[5] Ibid.

God understands that people think mostly about their basic needs, and as Rick Warren notes, even his various names reflect his understanding of reaching people through their needs. Warren writes:

> God's response has been to reveal himself according to what they needed at that specific time:
>
> [to] those who needed a miracle, God revealed himself as Jehovah-Jireh ("I am your provider")
>
> to those who needed comfort, God revealed himself as Jehovah-Shalom ("I am your peace")
>
> to those who needed salvation, God revealed himself as Jehovah-tsidkenu ("I am your righteousness").[6]

Find out which needs your audience finds most compelling, and tap into them. If you can connect your message via example or explanation to a person's deepest needs, you will win him or her over.

START WITH EXAMPLES YOUR AUDIENCE WILL UNDERSTAND

Occasionally we all have to communicate complex subject matter to people with little interest in or understanding of the concept at hand. Calculus teachers must reach high school students. Financial analysts must reach boards with short attention spans. Christians must reach non-Christians.

No matter what your subject, always start with an example or concept your audience knows, understands, or finds interesting, and connect it to your core message.

Consider Jesus' predicament: he was attempting to communicate a compelling message about the nature of the human predicament to fishermen, tax collectors, and prostitutes. That is why he used so many parables connecting familiar, concrete subjects to unfamiliar, abstract ones. In Matthew 7 alone he uses three simple, everyday examples (narrow and wide gates, a tree and its fruits, and foolish builders) to illuminate for people like you and me lessons

[6]Ibid.

about sin and salvation. The New Testament is crammed with similar examples, and you have seen good speakers do this outside the Bible as well. It's why they almost always introduce complex topics with humorous or heartwarming examples.

Know your audience, and start with the things *they* know.

SPEAK YOUR AUDIENCE'S LANGUAGE

It is important to speak your audience's language. Imagine for a moment what would happen if a concert pianist with no interest in sports was forced to host *Monday Night Football* by himself at the last minute. The man has no knowledge of football terminology, the two teams playing, or the rules of the game. His only metaphors and anecdotes involve classical music, and he speaks in a slow, understated voice. It would be a disaster.

When you speak to an audience, to the extent possible, you must speak their language. Jesus mastered this. When facing the Pharisees, he could quote Scripture. When facing the common people, he could speak to their needs and the situations with which they were familiar. Prostitutes and tax collectors liked Jesus because he knew how to talk to them, he knew what they needed, and he seemed to care about them.

In a more striking example, Acts 2 records how the disciples literally spoke in a multitude of languages on the Day of Pentecost so that all the people in the city could understand them. This kind of linguistic feat may not be possible for you, but you can actively seek to learn about your audience and brush up on the best ways to connect with them.

NEVER SPEAK ABOUT YOUR SPEECH

Some rhetorical concepts are best illustrated by their absence from Christ's rhetoric.

Have you ever watched a speaker who constantly talked about his speech during his speech? Did he reference how much time he would be talking or the fact that he was running long? Did she talk about the quality of the speech or lack thereof? Did he make a mistake and talk for several minutes about that mistake?

More often than not, these things distract you from the content of the message. That's probably why Jesus almost never spoke about the speech he was giving (except to note important aspects of it—for example, "this is prophecy").

Avoid talking about the length or quality of your speech or presentation during that speech or presentation. Don't spend a lot of time referencing mistakes or glitches (unless you are *really* funny). More often than not, these things distract your audience and hurt your credibility.

USE WITNESSES

Any prosecuting attorney can tell you of the importance of eyewitness testimony in criminal proceedings. Similarly, witnesses can be essential to effective communication in a campaign to change hearts and minds. We noted this in the chapter on ethos, but it bears repeating.

The Gospel of John records this exchange between Jesus and the Pharisees:

> Again Jesus spoke to them, saying, "I am the light of the world. Whoever follows me will not walk in darkness, but will have the light of life."
>
> So the Pharisees said to him, "You are bearing witness about yourself; your testimony is not true."
>
> Jesus answered, "Even if I do bear witness about myself, my testimony is true, for I know where I came from and where I am going, but you do not know where I come from or where I am going. You judge according to the flesh; I judge no one. Yet even if I do judge, my judgment is true, for it is not I alone who judge, but I and the Father who sent me. In your Law it is written that the testimony of two people is true. I am the one who bears witness about myself, and the Father who sent me bears witness about me." (John 8:12–18)

Elsewhere the New Testament notes the importance of John the Baptist as a precursor to Jesus—witnessing about the coming Savior's divinity, purity, and power—and the crucial part the disciples played in disseminating eyewitness testimony of Jesus' miracles and resurrection (and not just his philosophy of life). Jesus considers the use of witnesses essential to the construction of an effective message based on narrative and ethos. Wherever possible, elicit testimonies.

COMMUNICATE WITH CONFIDENCE

Jesus was a humble man, but he spoke with authority and confidence. He was bold and audacious, and he commanded us to be the same.

Jesus responds to Nathanael's proclamation of his divinity by saying, "Because I said to you, 'I saw you under the fig tree,' do you believe? You will see greater things than these" (John 1:50). Acts 4:31 notes that the apostles "continued to speak the word of God with boldness." And the Gospel of Matthew notes that when Jesus spoke, "the crowds were astonished at his teaching, for he was teaching them as one who had authority, and not as their scribes" (7:28–29).

How do you feel when a speaker seems under-confident? How do you feel when someone constantly includes caveats in a business presentation? In general, you doubt that person, and his message loses impact.

Of course, there are times to soften your message and call out the fact that you might be wrong. You are not Jesus, and you won't always be right. But in general, if you have been given the stage to speak or write about something, speak or write with confidence, and invite others into a robust discussion of your presentation if there are things that must be questioned. You will thus gain credibility and impact.

GET IT RIGHT

If you are going to speak with confidence, you should be right. You have to thoroughly know your subject to gain and maintain credibility.

Jesus performed miracles, prophesied, and made note of the

prophecies that he fulfilled to prove his audacious claims to divinity. In John 13:19 Jesus says of one of his prophecies, "I am telling you this now, before it takes place, that when it does take place you may believe that I am he."

Even before he began his ministry, he proved both his knowledge of Jewish law and prophecy and his affinity for an understanding of that tradition by reading and spending time in the Temple. Luke 2:46–47 notes that when Jesus disappeared for a time as a young child, his parents "found him in the temple, sitting among the teachers, listening to them and asking them questions" and that "all who heard him were amazed at his understanding and his answers." Jesus, from the time of his youth, had sufficient scholarly knowledge to be called "rabbi" (teacher) and prophesied only that which would come true.

When you are going to speak on a topic, debate with someone, or make a presentation, take the time to do your homework. Carefully study your topic, and build a solid reputation for knowing your subject. Take the time to fact-check and draw insightful conclusions. If you are consistently or frequently wrong, people will begin to doubt you, and your confidence will be taken as arrogance and bluster.

DO NOT BOAST; ACT WITH HUMILITY

Benjamin Franklin once said, "To be humble to superiors is duty, to equals courtesy, and to inferiors nobleness." As noted in the chapter on ethos, you should speak with confidence, but you should never boast. On all occasions strive to be to be seen as humble.

Jesus was the living incarnation of God, and though he openly stated his equality with the Father, he never boasted about it. He expected the same attitude from his followers, admonishing his listeners and disciples to be humble.

In Matthew 23:11–12 Jesus says, "The greatest among you shall be your servant. Whoever exalts himself will be humbled, and whoever humbles himself will be exalted." In Mark 9, the disciples are arguing "about who was the greatest," and Jesus scolds them by responding, "If anyone would be first, he must be last of all and servant of all" (vv. 34–35). With respect to giving to the needy, Jesus said, "Beware of practicing your righteousness before other people in order to be seen by them, for then you will have no reward from your Father who is in heaven" (Matthew 6:1). He also admonished his disciples, "And when you pray, you must not be like the hypocrites. For they love to stand and pray in the synagogues and at the street corners, that they may be seen by others" (Matthew 6:5). Whenever he spoke of his own actions, he was sure to note that he was doing what he had to do on earth for the glory of the Father.

Learn from Jesus' example. Give others credit where credit is due. Never talk about yourself or do charitable or noble things to impress people. It is morally wrong to do so, and it will only make your audience respect you less.

KNOW WHEN TO SPEAK AND WHEN TO BE SILENT

Silence is one of the most powerful forms of communication. In reading the Gospels, two counterintuitive elements of Jesus' communication leap out of the text. First, for the all-knowing God of the universe, Jesus asked a lot of questions. Second, Jesus used intentional silence at critical moments.

When Christ talked, he was clear and concise. He listened to his audience and chose his topics carefully. One imagines that Jesus could have formulated an intelligent opinion on anything; but he refrained from speaking more than was necessary. For instance, when confronted with a question about the competing claims of God and Caesar on a person's resources, Jesus simply responded, "Render to Caesar the things that are Caesar's, and to God the things that are God's" (Matthew 22:21).

Follow Jesus' example by knowing when to speak. Don't overreach. There are a lot of important topics in the world, and it is not necessary that you have something to say about all of them—particularly if speaking on the topic would hurt your credibility or detract from your primary goal. Be clear and concise, and don't speak just to hear your own voice. Speak to educate, relate, persuade, or entertain. Also, as noted elsewhere in this chapter, listen to people.

Jesus knew both when to speak and when to be silent. He was

often silent at critical moments, which increased the impact or urgency of the situation. Throughout the Gospels, we see dramatic moments when Jesus could have spoken eloquently but remained quiet instead. Consider that fateful moment when he was brought before Pilate. Having spoken with both Christ and the Jews a first time, Pilate goes out to tell the crowd he can find no fault with the man and wants nothing to do with his crucifixion. The religious leaders respond negatively. As the Gospel of John portrays the scene:

> The Jews answered him, "We have a law, and according to that law he ought to die because he has made himself the Son of God."
>
> When Pilate heard this statement, he was even more afraid. He entered his headquarters again and said to Jesus, "Where are you from?" But Jesus gave him no answer. So Pilate said to him, "You will not speak to me? Do you not know that I have authority to release you and authority to crucify you?"
>
> Jesus answered him, "You would have no authority over me at all unless it had been given you from above. Therefore he who delivered me over to you has the greater sin."
>
> From then on Pilate sought to release him, but the Jews cried out, "If you release this man, you are not Caesar's friend. Everyone who makes himself a king opposes Caesar." (John 19:7–12)

Jesus communicated profoundly with his silence. In Pilate's eyes, Christ was a Jew and a criminal who should be pleading with him for mercy. But Jesus was silent in the face of death, and his sense of authority and control frightened Pilate. It is doubtful that Pilate believed Jesus was the Son of God. But his refusal to respond likely frightened the ruler more than any affirmation or denial could have.

You can use silence to similar effect. It shows that you are in control and gives your audience a moment to think for themselves and consider how they will respond to your message. Silence can also be used to reinforce the importance of a message. When you have delivered a particularly important point, pause for a few moments while your audience assimilates the information. In the heat of a particularly livid debate, with both sides shouting back and forth, a moment of silence can change the direction of the conversation. Look for ways that you can use intentional silence to benefit your communication.

BE ENIGMATIC

Everyone loves a little mystery. It excites us and keeps us interested. If you are able to retain an air of mystery, people will be more drawn to you and will give more weight to your words.

Jesus was careful to keep some mystery around his actions, identity, and rhetoric. The Gospel of Luke records an interesting interaction between Jesus and the Pharisees:

> One day, as Jesus was teaching the people in the temple and preaching the gospel, the chief priests and the scribes with the elders came up and said to him, "Tell us by what authority you do these things, or who it is that gave you this authority."
>
> He answered them, "I also will ask you a question. Now tell me, was the baptism of John from heaven or from man?"
>
> And they discussed it with one another, saying, "If we say, 'From heaven,' he will say, 'Why did you not believe him?' But if we say, 'From man,' all the people will stone us to death, for they are convinced that John was a prophet." So they answered that they did not know where it came from.
>
> And Jesus said to them, "Neither will I tell you by what authority I do these things." (Luke 20:1–8)

Jesus made a number of ambiguous statements and was alternately coy and forthright about his divinity, the source of his power, the time of his crucifixion, and the hour of his return. While he gave people the clarity they needed, he also provided them with enough mystery to keep them interested.

We live in a "tell all" age in which people reveal every detail of their personal lives to strangers on the Internet. If you want to be an effective communicator, clarity is important. People have to understand you and know where you're coming from. But cultivating a little mystery can also have benefits.

LISTEN

Jesus Christ was a brilliant listener—not just because he asked questions and allowed his responders to answer them, but because he really took the time to hear and understand what people were saying. Christ heard not only what people asked or told him, but what they meant by their questions and comments. This had two primary effects. It made people take him seriously and care for him, and it allowed him to avoid traps that people would set for him.

Being a genuine listener often leads people to love and respect you. Take, for example, Jesus' encounter with a Canaanite woman in the Gospel of Matthew:

> And behold, a Canaanite woman from that region came out and was crying, "Have mercy on me, O Lord, Son of David; my daughter is severely oppressed by a demon."
>
> But he did not answer her a word. And his disciples came and begged him, saying, "Send her away, for she is crying out after us." He answered, "I was sent only to the lost sheep of the house of Israel." But she came and knelt before him, saying, "Lord, help me."
>
> And he answered, "It is not right to take the children's bread and throw it to the dogs."
>
> She said, "Yes, Lord, yet even the dogs eat the crumbs that fall from their masters' table."
>
> Then Jesus answered her, "O woman, great is your faith! Be it done for you as you desire." And her daughter was healed instantly. (Matthew 15:22–28)

Jesus' reputation was at least partially founded on instances like these. When others would ignore people's cries, Jesus would listen. And whereas the outcasts in society despised the religious order of the day, they loved Christ because he listened to them and cared for them.

Listening carefully also allowed Christ to understand people's comments and questions and to avoid traps or cultural biases. In a discussion with Jesus in the Gospel of Luke, a Pharisee correctly identifies "Love . . . your neighbor as yourself" as one of the things he must do to inherit eternal life, but then follows with the question, "And who is my neighbor?" (Luke 10:25–29).

As author Andy Stanley, pastor of North Point Community Church near Atlanta, has noted, Jesus realized that the Pharisee was trying to justify his own life and was missing the point of the parable: everyone is your neighbor, and everyone deserves love by simple virtue of his or her creation in the image of God. So instead of answering with a complex set of rules for identifying neighbors, Jesus answers with the Parable of the Good Samaritan and asks the question, "Which of these three, do you think, proved to be a neighbor to the man who fell among the robbers?" (v. 36). Instead of answering the way the Pharisee wanted him to, he answered the question the Pharisee should have asked: what does it mean to be a neighbor? Doing that requires really listening to those with whom we communicate.

ASK QUESTIONS

Few rhetorical tools are as effective as well-placed questions. In many passages in the Gospels, Jesus asks questions. Jesus' trial before the Jewish high priest provides a compelling example:

> The high priest then questioned Jesus about his disciples and his teaching.
>
> Jesus answered him, "I have spoken openly to the world. I have always taught in synagogues and in the temple, where all Jews come together. I have said nothing in secret. Why do you ask me? Ask those who have heard me what I said to them; they know what I said."
>
> When he had said these things, one of the officers standing by struck Jesus with his hand, saying, "Is that how you answer the high priest?"
>
> Jesus answered him, "If what I said is wrong, bear witness about the wrong; but if what I said is right, why do you strike me?" (John 18:19–23)

The types of questions Jesus asked varied broadly. Sometimes Jesus' questions were general; other times they were specific. Sometimes they were rhetorical, and sometimes they were meant to be answered. Jesus realized that there are numerous benefits to questions. They are often perceived as less aggressive or confrontational than statements or accusations. They make others think for themselves, involving them more deeply in the conversation. In some circumstances they elicit much-needed clarification. They can also force others to justify their own statements.

When in doubt, ask a question.

JUST ASK

If you wish to receive, then ask. We all have certain friends who frustrate us by their willingness to ask for what they want. We see them as nags, but they get better jobs, better seats at football games, and better deals on cell phones. Invariably, that is because they have the audacity to ask for what they want when they want it the way they want it, and they do not give up without a clear "No!"

Surprisingly, Jesus seemed to favor this mentality. In Matthew 7:7 Jesus says, "Ask, and it will be given to you; seek, and you will find; knock, and it will be opened to you." Concerning prayer, Jesus tells us to be like an elderly widow petitioning an unjust judge until he exclaims in exasperation, "Though I neither fear God nor respect man, yet because this widow keeps bothering me, I will give her justice, so that she will not beat me down by her continual coming" (Luke 18:4–5).

While these passages relate specifically to prayer, we believe there is a broader message. You won't get anything without asking. There are times to be subtle, but other times it pays just to ask.

WHEN APPROPRIATE, STAND UP TO AUTHORITY

Sometimes it is rhetorically and morally proper to oppose authority, whether that authority be the will of an individual or the will of a crowd.

Jesus often found himself in opposition to authority. He regularly condemned the hypocrisy and legalism of the religious leaders, and he often found himself in conflict with the opinion of the crowd. At the end of his life, he even found himself opposed to the power of Rome, as manifested in Pilate. In all of these circumstances, he opposed one authority (an earthly authority) out of dedication to a higher authority (God). And when he took a stand, it had a strong rhetorical impact.

In John 8:44, Jesus referred to a crowd of people as children of the devil and promptly roused the anger of that crowd. In Mark 11:15, Jesus physically chased money-changers from the temple, revoking their authority because of the preexisting authority of God. And in his confrontation with Pilate, Jesus told the magistrate that the magistrate had no authority over him except that which was granted by God (John 19:11).

In their day-to-day lives, most people obey the governing authorities and suffer what they must to endure their rule. But there is something in human nature that is passionately roused (for good or ill) by opposition to authority. As a communicator, use this opposition carefully, when you are morally and rhetorically compelled to do so.

DON'T BEND CORE PRINCIPLES OR STANDARDS TO GATHER DISCIPLES

In the process of recruiting disciples for a message or cause, it is tempting to water down your main points to attract a wider pool of people. But it is clear from the Gospels that Jesus believed this to be the wrong approach. While he encouraged Christians to be tolerant and open to others, he required his disciples to adhere to core concepts.

John 6 notes the grumbling among the disciples after Jesus delivered a hard message, but Christ refused to compromise the message.

> But Jesus, knowing in himself that his disciples were grumbling about this, said to them, "Do you take offense at this? Then what if you were to see the Son of Man ascending to where he was before? It is the Spirit who gives life; the flesh is no help at all. The words that I have spoken to you are spirit and life. But there are some of you who do not believe." (For Jesus knew from the beginning who those were who did not believe, and who it was who would betray him.) And he said, "This is why I told you that no one can come to me unless it is granted him by the Father." After this many of his disciples turned back and no longer walked with him. (John 6:61–66)

Elsewhere Jesus encourages believers who have consistently confronted other believers about sin to expel them from the group, saying, "But if he does not listen, take one or two others along with you, that every charge may be established by the evidence of two or three witnesses. If he refuses to listen to them, tell it to the church. And if he refuses to listen even to the church, let him be to you as a Gentile and a tax collector" (Matthew 18:16–17).

The message is clear. On core principles you have to stay firm to preserve the integrity of the message and the credibility of those relaying it. You don't want someone to corrupt a movement from the inside or co-opt a message for his or her own purposes.

CREATE A SENSE OF URGENCY

When you want to persuade people to act quickly, you must generate a sense of urgency. Jesus demonstrated this in several ways, primarily by noting the fleeting nature of his time on earth and the impending approach of judgment.

Speaking to the disciples in John 13:33, Jesus says, "Little children, yet a little while I am with you. You will seek me, and just as I said to the Jews, so now I also say to you, 'Where I am going you cannot come.'" Jesus' statement reminds the disciples that they will soon be separated, presumably increasing the urgency with which they assimilate the information he is passing on to them.

Similarly, in Matthew 24:42–44 Jesus says of his return, "Therefore, stay awake, for you do not know on what day your Lord is coming. But know this, that if the master of the house had known in what part of the night the thief was coming, he would have stayed awake and would not have let his house be broken into. Therefore you also must be ready, for the Son of Man is coming at an hour you do not expect."

If you want people to act quickly, you must demonstrate that the time for action is upon them. Creating a sense of urgency in those you hope to persuade can be as essential as demonstrating to them the ways in which they can act.

REMEMBER, A PROPHET IS WITHOUT HONOR IN HIS HOMETOWN

Mark 6:4 records Jesus' words, "A prophet is not without honor, except in his hometown and among his relatives and in his own household."

Sometimes it is in the very place that we need the most respect and encouragement that we receive the least. As a communicator, you will want your friends and family to accept and praise you; but those closest to you will often be the toughest sell. They've seen your faults and hypocrisies. They know what you look like unshaven and groggy. They've seen you when you were angry and irrational. It may be hard to communicate with them in the same way that you communicate with others.

Even Jesus had this problem. Earlier verses in Mark 6 record that when Jesus spoke in his hometown, the crowd responded skeptically, saying, "Where did this man get these things? What is the wisdom given to him? How are such mighty works done by his hands? Is not this the carpenter, the son of Mary and brother of James and Joses and Judas and Simon? And are not his sisters here with us?" (vv. 2–3). At some point we all face a similar problem. Remember that you are in good company.

PRAISE THOSE WHO DO WELL; EXPRESS DISAPPOINTMENT IN THOSE WHO DISAPPOINT YOU

Communicators generally fall into two camps—those who praise and comfort their audiences without exception and those who only criticize their audiences. If you want to communicate like Jesus, you must both praise people for the things they do well and criticize them when they disappoint.

In Jesus' Parable of the Talents, he relates the story of a master who leaves town and gives money to several of his servants for safekeeping. When the master returns, he compliments the servants who have multiplied the money he left them, saying, "Well done, good and faithful servant. You have been faithful over a little; I will set you over much. Enter into the joy of your master" (Matthew 25:21,

23). But to the servant who did not multiply his master's money the master replies, "You wicked and slothful servant! You knew that I reap where I have not sown and gather where I scattered no seed? Then you ought to have invested my money with the bankers, and at my coming I should have received what was my own with interest" (vv. 26–27).

Clearly, if the master in this parable is meant to represent God, he is not a God preeminently concerned with self-esteem. Indeed, throughout the Gospels Jesus confronts disciples who disappoint him (like Judas and Peter), even if he subsequently forgives them for their failures.

At work, home, or school, no one benefits if your compliments are meaningless or excessive. Nor do people benefit when you refuse to acknowledge their successes. Mix deserved congratulation with constructive criticism, and people will both take your opinion seriously and strive to please you.

DON'T FEAR DIVISION

Christ's purpose on earth was to call people to repentance and salvation and to provide them with the means of that salvation. But he didn't mind causing division for the right reasons.

In Luke 12:49–53 he says:

> "I came to cast fire on the earth, and would that it were already kindled! I have a baptism to be baptized with, and how great is my distress until it is accomplished! Do you think that I have come to give peace on earth? No, I tell you, but rather division. For from now on in one house there will be five divided, three against two and two against three. They will be divided, father against son and son against father, mother against daughter and daughter against mother, mother-in-law against her daughter-in-law and daughter-in-law against mother-in-law."

Whenever possible, you should seek to unite, not divide. And in most circumstances it is better to compromise with those who oppose your message than to place the purity of your goals over the practicality of forward progress. But sometimes it is essential that you do not compromise in your communications. Be discerning. If the situation calls for you to make a moral stand, do not fear dividing your audience for good reason. In some situations bright lines are both useful and necessary.

DON'T CAST YOUR PEARLS BEFORE SWINE

In Matthew 7:6 Jesus delivers one of his most memorable lines: "Do not give dogs what is holy, and do not throw your pearls before pigs, lest they trample them underfoot and turn to attack you."

In context, this phrase is clearly meant to limit the time we spend communicating with or attempting to disciple those who have absolutely no appreciation for our efforts.

In the broad rhetorical context, it is easy to spend all of your efforts trying to persuade those who disagree with you, despise you, attack you, or condescend to you. On blogs you can get caught in endless battles with trolls (those who intentionally post messages about sensitive topics just to cause controversy). As a teacher you can find yourself spending all of your time and effort on "problem children" and little effort on those curious children who are excited about school. In business you can take disproportionate amounts of your time to influence naysayers and end up losing the enthusiasm and support of everyone else.

Jesus noted that there is a time to evaluate the impact you are having and to direct your time and energy toward receptive, curious, or open people. Don't cast your pearls before swine.

WORDS MATTER

In the chapter on ethos, we highlighted the fact that actions sometimes speak more loudly than words. Likewise, in the section on narrative and imagery we noted the necessity of a human example for the messages you hope to communicate. But none of these admonitions should reduce the importance of one very simple fact: words matter. Words are at the center of the human experience, and oral and visual communications can have untold impact on the realities of the world around us.

There is no better example of the preeminence of communication than the first chapter of the Gospel of John. In it, Jesus' beloved disciple writes:

> In the beginning was the Word, and the Word was with God, and the Word was God. He was in the beginning with God. . . . And the Word became flesh and dwelt among us, and we have seen his glory, glory as of the only Son from the Father, full of grace and truth. (John 1:1–2, 14)

John's metaphor is monumental. The importance of human language, and therefore human communication, is impossible to exaggerate. There is a reason Christ spoke his sermons. There is a reason God chose to reveal himself over several millennia via the written word. Our ability to communicate is in some sense a way in which we participate in the divine. Even nonreligious scholars have admitted the importance of human language as a differentiator between humans and other complex beings. Noted linguist Noam Chomsky once wrote:

> Even the most superficial observation suffices to show that there are qualitative differences between humans and other complex organisms which must be explained. If our hypothetical Martian observer searches a bit further, he will find that human beings are unique in many respects, one of these being their ability to acquire a rich and varied linguistic system, which can be used freely and in the most subtle and complicated ways, merely by immersion in a linguistic community in which the system is used.[7]

Effective communication is not just another parlor trick. It is a way in which everyday people can imitate the example of Christ and change the world.

[7]Noam Chomsky, "Empiricism and Rationalism," *Language and Responsibility* (New York: Pantheon, 1977); http://www.chomsky.info/books/responsibility02.htm.

CONCEPT REVIEW

Heuristic: A "rule of thumb" that while not universally applicable can be a pragmatic tool for evaluating the right course of action in a given situation.

QUESTIONS FOR FURTHER CONSIDERATION

1. What heuristics would you add to this list? Are there any that seem incorrect?
2. What heuristics do you use in everyday life? Who taught them to you?
3. Is there someone you admire? Does he or she seem to operate based on a collection of heuristics?
4. Think of a recent conversation, speech, or presentation that went poorly. Would any of these heuristics have been helpful to you in that situation?
5. Heuristics are rules of thumb, not universal principles. It is important, therefore, that we are discerning when following them. Think of a time you used a rule of thumb and it proved wrong. Why did things go badly? What might have helped you determine not to use that heuristic?

CHAPTER SEVEN

CASE STUDIES

CASE 1: *OTHER PEOPLE'S MONEY*

Source: *Other People's Money*, a 1991 film directed by Norman Jewison based on an off-Broadway play by Jerry Sterner.

Setting: Andrew "Jorgy" Jorgenson (Gregory Peck) is the warmhearted patriarch of an old "mom and pop" business, New England Wire and Cable, that has grown substantially to include outside shareholders. One of the company's core businesses is failing because its product is becoming technologically obsolete. Wall Street corporate raider Larry "The Liquidator" Garfield (played by Danny DeVito) descends on the business with the intention of buying up the company stock so he can break up the company and sell off its assets.

In one of the final scenes, each man gives a speech to the shareholders to persuade them to vote for or against the takeover.

First Speaker: Andrew "Jorgy" Jorgenson, chairman of New England Wire and Cable Company.

Speech:

> Well, it's good to see so many familiar faces, so many old friends. Some of you I haven't seen in years. Well thank you for coming. Now, Bill Coles, our able President, in the annual report has told you of our year, of what we accomplished, of the need for further improvements, our business goals for next year and the years beyond. I'd like to talk to you about something else. I wanna share with you some of my thoughts concerning the vote that you're gonna make and the company that you own.
>
> This proud company, which has survived the death of its founder, numerous recessions, one major depression, and two world wars is in imminent danger of self-destructing—on this day,

in the town of its birth. There is the instrument of our destruction. I want you to look at him in all of his glory, Larry "The Liquidator," the entrepreneur of post-industrial America, playing God with other people's money. The Robber Barons of old at least left something tangible in their wake—a coal mine, a railroad, banks. This man leaves nothing. He creates nothing. He builds nothing. He runs nothing. And in his wake lies nothing but a blizzard of paper to cover the pain.

Oh, if he said, "I know how to run your business better than you," that would be something worth talking about. But he's not saying that. He's saying, "I'm going to kill you because at this particular moment in time, you're worth more dead than alive." Well, maybe that's true, but it is also true that one day this industry will turn. One day when the yen is weaker, the dollar is stronger—or when we finally begin to rebuild our roads, our bridges, the infrastructure of our country—demand will skyrocket. And when those things happen, we will still be here, stronger because of our ordeal, stronger because we have survived. And the price of our stock will make his offer pale by comparison. God save us if we vote to take his paltry few dollars and run. God save this country if that is truly the wave of the future. We will then have become a nation that makes nothing but hamburgers, creates nothing but lawyers, and sells nothing but tax shelters. And if we are at that point in this country, where we kill something because at the moment it's worth more dead than alive—well, take a look around.

Look at your neighbor. You won't kill him, will you? No. It's called murder and it's illegal. Well, this too is murder—on a mass scale. Only on Wall Street, they call it "maximizing share-holder value" and they call it "legal." And they substitute dollar bills where a conscience should be. [expletive deleted] A business is worth more than the price of its stock. It's the place where we earn our living, where we meet our friends, dream our dreams. It is, in every sense, the very fabric that binds our society together. So let us now, at this meeting, say to every Garfield in the land, "Here, we build things. We don't destroy them. Here, we care about more than the price of our stock! Here, we care about people."[1]

[1] *Other People's Money*, directed by Norman Jewison, starring Gregory Peck and Danny DeVito, Warner Bros., 1991; www.americanrhetoric.com/MovieSpeeches/moviespeechotherpeoplesmoneypeck.html.

ANALYSIS

Logos

Jorgenson lists two reasons why the current price of the stock is deflated (the yen is stronger than the dollar; current lack of demand), presumably basing the thrust of his larger argument on some factual foundation. From this he develops an extended *syllogismus* ("One day . . . our stock will make his offer pale by comparison") that relies on the shareholders agreeing with his reasoning.

In addition, Jorgenson builds logical arguments with short enthymemes or *syllogismuses* that rely on assumptions he believes are shared by the other stockholders. Setting up the contrast between "building" (like him) and "destroying" (like Larry) as a means of creating value, he relies on a sense among his shareholders that "building" as he characterizes it is the better long-term value maximization strategy both for the company and for the community.

He also relies on a syllogistic argument about the real value of business, stating, "a business is worth more than the price of its stock." He assumes shareholders agree with him that the value of the business to the community is just as important as its financial value to the shareholders and that the community is better served with New England Wire and Cable than with whatever might replace it. In doing so, he builds a cumulative case. He first argues that in the long term, it is more value-maximizing to maintain the business. Then he argues that even if that were not true, the business has such a high and irreplaceable value to the community that it should be maintained even if it is not more profitable to keep it.

Pathos

Jorgenson's appeal rests on pathos more than logos, and he employs many of the tools of pathos we've discussed so far.

> *Shared values:* Jorgenson appeals to the shareholders' sense of community, asking them to put people ahead of the price of the stock. Relying on the fact that people would rather be "builders" than "destroyers" and that they would rather be seen as long-term rather than short-term thinkers, Jorgenson appeals to their values by aligning

himself with a long-term outlook and a strategy of building things up rather than tearing them down.

Shared artifacts: Jorgenson's advantage over Garfield is that he has weathered all of the company's storms along with it and its shareholders, and he is familiar with the artifacts of the company. In many ways, he is an artifact of the company. The chairman recites the hardships that the company, the community, the employees, and the shareholders have gone through together ("This proud company, which has survived the death of its founder, numerous recessions, one major depression, and two world wars is in imminent danger of self-destructing—on this day, in the town of its birth").

Energia: After allowing the company's president to give the dry, impersonal details of the business, Jorgenson counterbalances the annual report by giving an emotional appeal. This is difficult to tell from the script, but his speech is quite passionate and energetic. While it starts quietly, the speech builds to a crescendo of exclamations.

Repetition: The speech uses *ploce*, repeating synonyms for death and destruction ten times (" . . . death . . . self-destructing . . . destruction . . . kill . . . dead . . . kill . . . dead . . . kill . . . murder . . . destroy . . .") in order to establish the dire straits in which Garfield would place the company.

Ethos

One of Jorgenson's primary perceived weapons against Garfield is his credibility with the shareholders. He knows them. He has weathered all of the company's storms and successes with them; and he is seen as a pillar of the community—someone who can be trusted to have the best interests of the business and the community in mind.

In reciting facts about the company, he calls to mind that he himself has been an essential part of the company. In speaking ill of Garfield ("This man leaves nothing. He creates nothing. He builds nothing. He *runs* nothing"), he simultaneously seeks to injure Garfield's credibility and, by contrast, enhance his own, implicitly arguing that he possesses the opposite of those negative qualities and relying on his established ethos to convince the shareholders. Finally he even seems to rely on the idea that he is so respected, the shareholders want to be like him and so will seek to share his values. In the last paragraph he asks them to embrace the values of the country (implicitly, his values) and reject those of "Wall Street" by adopting what he defines as a kind of others-first mind-set that places creation and community ahead of self-interest.

Narrative and Imagery

Finally, Jorgenson's setting up his speech with an abbreviated account of the business serves to highlight the long record of the company, placing it within the context of America's history. He also implies that he is a leader from the age of industry ("Here, we *build* things"), unlike Garfield, "the entrepreneur of post-industrial America" ("We don't destroy them. Here, we care about more than the price of our stock!"), highlighting the divergence by depicting Garfield's ideology with imagery of murder and destruction. By standing up to Garfield, they are deciding that this narrative will continue ("So let us now, at this meeting, say to every Garfield in the land . . .") as it is rather than sliding into an unappealing tale of deception, superficiality, and destruction.

As you may agree, Jorgenson's message is strong, and if you are familiar with the work of Gregory Peck, you know that it is delivered forcefully and authoritatively. Within the context of the film, it looks as if there is no way for Garfield to respond.

Second Speaker: Larry "The Liquidator" Garfield, corporate raider.

Speech:

> Amen. And amen. And amen. You have to forgive me. I'm not familiar with the local custom. Where I come from, you always say "Amen" after you hear a prayer. Because that's what you just heard—a prayer. Where I come from, that particular prayer is called "The Prayer for the Dead." You just heard The Prayer for the Dead, my fellow stockholders, and you didn't say, "Amen."
>
> This company is dead. I didn't kill it. Don't blame me. It was dead when I got here. It's too late for prayers. For even if the prayers were answered, and a miracle occurred, and the yen did this, and the dollar did that, and the infrastructure did the other thing, we would still be dead. You know why? Fiber optics. New

technologies. Obsolescence. We're dead alright. We're just not broke. And you know the surest way to go broke? Keep getting an increasing share of a shrinking market. Down the tubes. Slow but sure.

You know, at one time there must've been dozens of companies makin' buggy whips. And I'll bet the last company around was the one that made the best [expletive deleted] buggy whip you ever saw. Now how would you have liked to have been a stockholder in that company? You invested in a business and this business is dead. Let's have the intelligence, let's have the decency to sign the death certificate, collect the insurance, and invest in something with a future.

"Ah, but we can't," goes the prayer. "We can't because we have responsibility, a responsibility to our employees, to our community. What will happen to them?" I got two words for that: Who cares? Care about them? Why? They didn't care about you. They sucked you dry. You have no responsibility to them. For the last ten years this company bled your money. Did this community ever say, "We know times are tough. We'll lower taxes, reduce water and sewer"? Check it out: You're paying twice what you did ten years ago. And our devoted employees, who have taken no increases for the past three years, are still making twice what they made ten years ago; and our stock—one-sixth what it was ten years ago.

Who cares? I'll tell ya: Me. I'm not your best friend. I'm your only friend. I don't make anything? I'm makin' you money. And lest we forget, that's the only reason any of you became stockholders in the first place. You wanna make money! You don't care if they manufacture wire and cable, fried chicken, or grow tangerines! You wanna make money! I'm the only friend you've got. I'm makin' you money.

Take the money. Invest it somewhere else. Maybe, maybe you'll get lucky and it'll be used productively. And if it is, you'll create new jobs and provide a service for the economy and even make a few bucks for yourselves. And if anybody asks, tell 'em ya gave at the plant.

And by the way, it pleases me that I am called "Larry the Liquidator." You know why, fellow stockholders? Because at my funeral, you'll leave with a smile on your face and a few bucks in your pocket. Now that's a funeral worth having![2]

---

[2]See www.americanrhetoric.com/MovieSpeeches/moviespeechotherpeoplesmoneydevito.html.

ANALYSIS

Narrative and Imagery

Garfield's response is brilliant first and foremost because he realizes that he does not have the ethos to beat Jorgenson on his home turf and that no amount of logos or pathos will counteract Jorgenson's within the context of the narrative he provided. So Garfield's first step is to discredit Jorgenson's narrative and completely replace it with a narrative of his own. Garfield realizes that Jorgenson has created a context within which he may not be able to win. So he creates a new story from the ashes of Jorgenson's "dead" one that plays to Garfield's ethos and the strengths of his own logical and emotional arguments.

First, Garfield, completely unfazed by Jorgenson's heart-wrenching appeal, mocks that appeal, referring to it as a silly prayer of desperation. Garfield energetically exclaims, "Amen. And amen. And amen." Then he refers to Jorgenson's speech not just as a prayer but as a prayer for the dead. There his story begins.

Whereas Jorgenson's narrative was one of a tried and tested company soldiering valiantly through yet another minor setback, Garfield's story is of a once strong company made obsolete (like its founder) by age and time. Garfield, depicted as a murderer in Jorgenson's narrative, establishes himself rather as a mere mortician who is there to salvage a little value and dignity from an already dead business.

Even more than Jorgenson, he makes this narrative utterly pervasive and reinforces it with brilliant imagery. He embraces the derisive term "Larry the Liquidator" and makes it a positive one, then closes his speech with the imagery of a funeral and offers the shareholders a seemingly more pleasant option than the unsightly prolonged struggle implicit in Jorgenson's plan: "[A]t my funeral, you'll leave with a smile on your face and a few bucks in your pocket. Now that's a funeral worth having!"

Logos

Garfield's logical arguments are subtle, buried within his larger narrative. First, he tries to argue that Jorgenson's argument for persistence and creation has its limits and that both reason and the facts of the case bear out the idea that companies can die and that when they do it is best to let them die and move on to new endeavors.

By citing the example of buggy whip makers, a business that became obsolete when buggies were irrevocably replaced by motor vehicles, appealing to evidence ("fiber optics," etc.), claiming that New England Wire and Cable faces a similar technological obsolescence, he doesn't even have to complete the argument—the shareholders complete it for him. Just as buggy whip makers eventually had to die gracefully, so must wire and cable manufacturers.

Second, Garfield argues that shareholders' primary logical obligation is not to the community at large but to themselves, because the community has never cared about them:

> Who cares? Care about them? Why? They didn't care about you. They sucked you dry. You have no responsibility to them. For the last ten years this company bled your money. Did this community ever say, "We know times are tough. We'll lower taxes, reduce water and sewer"? Check it out: You're paying twice what you did ten years ago. And our devoted employees, who have taken no increases for the past three years, are still making twice what they made ten years ago; and our stock—one-sixth what it was ten years ago.

Garfield argues that care must be mutual to be worthwhile and the community has never demonstrated the same care and understanding Jorgenson is asking of the shareholders. Additionally, just like Jorgenson, he builds his own cumulative case, stating later in his speech that even if they do care for the community, liquidation of New England Wire and Cable is good for all parties involved. In doing so, he lays multiple supports for his argument and avoids the false dilemma established by Jorgenson:

> Take the money. Invest it somewhere else. Maybe, maybe you'll get lucky and it'll be used productively. And if it is, you'll create new jobs and provide a service for the economy and even make a few bucks for yourselves. And if anybody asks, tell 'em ya gave at the plant.

Finally, he uses *reductio ad absurdum*, in the guise of his "buggy whip" example, to show where Jorgenson's logic may lead New England Wire and Cable. Jorgenson's argument seemed strong. Garfield's makes it seem naive.

Pathos

Garfield's argument has incredible emotional appeal. Even more than Jorgenson he demonstrates *energia*, becoming impassioned and making repeated exclamations as he speaks. He seems passionate and joyful, breaking the solemnity of the occasion.

He also appeals to the shareholders' sense of shared values. He doesn't want them to value the community-mindedness proposed by Jorgenson and tears it down. Instead he appeals to their self-interest, arguing that his solution will protect their money, and that is the highest value in business. He argues, in parallel, that this will also lead to other favorable things like dignity and joy. And when he paints the company's current plight as a prolonged and somber funeral, he portrays his purchase of the company as a pleasant way out.

Relying on repetition, he uses the word "amen" five times in the first paragraph and introduces almost every new thought with the imagery of a prayer or a funeral—both of which are conventionally attached to feelings of sadness and dread (at least as portrayed here). To counter Jorgenson's shared artifacts—the bonds of community, persistence, creation, and struggle—he introduces other shared artifacts from that narrative that depict it in a different light. He points out that as the shareholders were building a community, the community rarely worked to benefit them. He mentions financial struggles that the shareholders endured with no sympathy from the larger community; and he pulls on other shared artifacts—like the death of buggy whip makers—to emphasize the ever-changing landscape of American business.

He asks sarcastic and leading questions, building a gradual anger in the shareholders toward the community and the supposed silliness of Jorgenson's appeal, and attempts to work them into outrage over the insistence by Jorgenson that they persist under traditional conditions rather than taking something of value for themselves.

Ethos

Finally, whereas Jorgenson relies on his ethos as a patriarch and community leader, Garfield relies on his ethos as a shrewd businessman and a reliable custodian of shareholder money. He knows that he is not as liked as Jorgenson, and he doesn't think that matters. His credibility is as a greedy investor, a money-maximizer, and he attempts to convince the shareholders that he, not a patriarch, is exactly what they need.

"You wanna make money!" Garfield exclaims. "I'm the only friend you've got. I'm makin' you money." He uses phrases like "fellow stockholders" to emphasize that he is a shareholder just like them; and throughout the speech he reframes "friend" to mean someone who understands and protects their true interests—someone like Larry the Liquidator.

Jorgenson came in with a solid narrative, decent logic, impeccable credibility, and a strong emotional appeal. Larry the Liquidator came in and reframed that narrative so effectively that Jorgenson's appeals were made largely irrelevant and he, Larry "The Liquidator" Garfield, arose as the new patriarch of New England Wire and Cable.

CASE STUDY QUESTIONS

1. Who do you think won the argument, Jorgenson or Garfield? Why? What line of argumentation was most persuasive to you?
2. The elements of speech we outlined above do not include every example of effective rhetoric listed in this book. What are some of the others?
3. Are there any obvious violations of the effective rhetoric listed in this book? What are they?
4. How might Jorgenson have strengthened his case and won the argument with Garfield, maintaining control of New England Wire and Cable?

5. Have you ever seen an example of a debate such as this? What was it? Who won the debate and why?

CASE 2: ROBERT F. KENNEDY'S SPEECH ON THE ASSASSINATION OF DR. MARTIN LUTHER KING JR.

Source: Text of Robert F. Kennedy's speech on the assassination of Martin Luther King Jr.[3]

Setting: On April 4, 1968, Robert F. Kennedy was to give a speech in an inner-city area of Indianapolis. Kennedy was working his way through the primary as a candidate for the Democratic presidential nomination when a short time before the speech he received word that Martin Luther King Jr. had been assassinated in Memphis. Kennedy took the stage in Indianapolis anyway and made a heartfelt, powerful plea for peace and unity. Riots broke out in approximately a hundred cities that night,[4] but not in Indianapolis. Some credit Indianapolis citizens' restraint, in part, to Kennedy's influence.[5]

Speech:

> Ladies and gentlemen, I'm only going to talk to you just for a minute or so this evening because I have some very sad news for all of you—could you lower those signs please?—I have some very sad news for all of you, and, I think, sad news for all of our fellow citizens, and people who love peace all over the world, and that is that Martin Luther King was shot and was killed tonight [screams from crowd].
>
> Martin Luther King dedicated his life to love and to justice between fellow human beings. He died in the cause of that effort.
>
> In this difficult day, in this difficult time for the United States, it is perhaps well to ask what kind of a nation we are and what direction we want to move in. For those of you who are black—considering the evidence evidently is, that there were white people who were responsible—you can be filled with bitterness, and with hatred, and a desire for revenge. We can move in that direc-

[3]See the PBS website; http://www.pbs.org/wgbh/amex/kennedys/filmmore/ps_indy.html.
[4]See BBC website; http://news.bbc.co.uk/onthisday/hi/dates/stories/april/4/newsid_2453000/2453987.stm.
[5]See http://www.indygov.org/eGov/Mayor/PR/2006/4/20060404b.htm.

tion as a country, in greater polarization—black people amongst blacks, and white amongst whites, filled with hatred toward one another.

Or we can make an effort, as Martin Luther King did, to understand, and to comprehend, and replace that violence, that stain of bloodshed that has spread across our land, with an effort to understand, compassion and love.

For those of you who are black and are tempted to be filled with hatred and mistrust of the injustice of such an act, against all white people, I would only say that I can also feel in my own heart the same kind of feeling. I had a member of my family killed, but he was killed by a white man. But we have to make an effort in the United States, we have to make an effort to understand, to get beyond or go beyond these rather difficult times.

My favorite poet was Aeschylus. And he once wrote: "Even in our sleep, pain which cannot forget falls drop by drop upon the heart until, in our own despair, against our will, comes wisdom through the awful grace of God."

What we need in the United States is not division; what we need in the United States is not hatred; what we need in the United States is not violence and lawlessness; but is love and wisdom, and compassion toward one another, and a feeling of justice toward those who still suffer within our country, whether they be white or whether they be black.

So I shall ask you tonight to return home, to say a prayer for the family of Martin Luther King, that's true, but more importantly, to say a prayer for our own country, which all of us love—a prayer for understanding and that compassion of which I spoke.

We can do well in this country. We will have difficult times; we've had difficult times in the past; and we will have difficult times in the future. It is not the end of violence; it is not the end of lawlessness; and it is not the end of disorder.

But the vast majority of white people and the vast majority of black people in this country want to live together, want to improve the quality of our life, and want justice for all human beings that abide in our land.

Dedicate ourselves to what the Greeks wrote so many years ago: to tame the savageness of man and make gentle the life of this world.

Let us dedicate ourselves to that, and say a prayer for our country and for our people.

ANALYSIS

Ethos

While it is not evident from the text, much of the power of Robert Kennedy's speech rested on his credibility as a sincere proponent of civil rights and an ally of Martin Luther King Jr. The 1960s were a difficult time for African-Americans. The institution of slavery still lingered in the form of segregated bathrooms, water fountains, and schools. It still lingered in the attitudes and actions of many whites. But Kennedy was a steadfast supporter of civil rights whom many in the black community trusted. He often campaigned in inner cities and beyond the U.S. He made trips to South Africa, where he spoke out against apartheid. He had powerful *eunoia*, or goodwill, with the audience. Adding to his personal credibility, Kennedy himself had gone through a similar tragedy and risen above it. In the speech, Kennedy notes:

> For those of you who are black and are tempted to be filled with hatred and mistrust of the injustice of such an act, against all white people, I would only say that I can also feel in my own heart the same kind of feeling. I had a member of my family killed, but he was killed by a white man. But we have to make an effort in the United States, we have to make an effort to understand, to get beyond or go beyond these rather difficult times.

Robert Kennedy's brother, President John F. Kennedy, had been assassinated earlier in the same decade, and his reference to the matter reminded his audience that he spoke from experience. His were not the shallow words of a pandering politician, but the heartfelt sentiments of a mourning brother and a crusader for the cause of civil rights.

In addition, his words carried powerful elements of *phronesis* (common sense) that King himself employed. He gently reminded the audience that they all shared in a similar struggle and that, as King implored, that struggle should soldier on as peacefully as possible. Borrowing the credibility of the martyr himself, Kennedy said, ". . . we can make an effort, as Martin Luther King did, to understand, and to comprehend, and replace that violence, that stain of bloodshed that has spread across our land, with an effort to understand, compassion and love." He used that credibility effectively to resonate with his audience and to counteract the urge that many of his listeners may have had to do violence to others.

Pathos

Of equal importance, Kennedy deftly employed pathos—particularly the pathos of shared values—in his speech.

Kennedy explicitly called out the shared aspirations held by the blacks in his audience and many of their white neighbors, saying, "the vast majority of white people and the vast majority of black people in this country want to live together, want to improve the quality of our life, and want justice for all human beings that abide in our land." Do those qualities resonate with you? Almost certainly they do, as they did with Kennedy's audience. And by appealing to his audience's fundamental aspirations Kennedy touched their hearts.

In addition, Kennedy combined both repetition and shared values in the following passage:

> What we need in the United States is not division; what we need in the United States is not hatred; what we need in the United States is not violence and lawlessness; but is love and wisdom, and compassion toward one another, and a feeling of justice toward those who still suffer within our country, whether they be white or whether they be black.

And he used the concept of *energia* to great effect—not by becoming overly passionate but by maintaining his composure in the midst of chaos and despair. His is an important lesson: sometimes understated emotion is more powerful than overdone passion.

Narrative and Imagery

Kennedy's is a short speech, but he did employ limited narrative and imagery.

Most broadly, he used narrative to call to mind the legacy of Martin Luther King, and in doing so he encouraged his audience to take part in that ongoing narrative of peaceful struggle and nonviolence. He refocused the audience's attention from politics to pain, suffering and the acquisition of wisdom, quoting the poet Aeschylus.

It was also with that quote that he introduced a brilliant piece of visual imagery: "Even in our sleep, pain which cannot forget falls drop by drop upon the heart until, in our own despair, against our will, comes wisdom through the awful grace of God." His words call to mind a steady flow of water eroding the soft outer layer of a piece of stone and leaving its hard core exposed. Later he once again refers to the Greeks, saying, "Dedicate ourselves to what the Greeks wrote so many years ago: to tame the savageness of man and make gentle the life of this world."

And, finally, the understated reference to the death of his own brother, John, even served as a short parable about the necessity of patience, struggle, and endurance. Rather than allowing himself to be overcome by grief, Robert Kennedy carried on, his beliefs only solidified by the tragedy, and listeners might infer his advice that they carry on in a similar way.

Logos

There is a subtle logic, founded on moral principles, throughout Kennedy's speech; but he knew better than to rely primarily on reason in a moment that called for emotion. The heart of this speech, appropriately, is pathos.

CASE STUDY QUESTIONS

1. What was the overall goal of Kennedy's speech? Was it accomplished?
2. What is the most powerful part of Kennedy's speech for you? Might different people be attracted to different portions of the speech?
3. What elements might Kennedy have expounded upon to make the speech even more powerful?
4. Have you ever been moved by a tragedy? Did the person or news outlet that delivered the news of that tragedy enhance its impact or alter your mood? What in their communication of the tragedy failed or succeeded in altering your mood or perspective?

GLOSSARY

***a fortiori*.** Latin, literally, "from the stronger"; a claim we are bound to accept because of our prior acceptance of a weaker application of the same reasoning or truth.

allegory. A figurative mode of representation conveying a meaning other than the literal.

***anamnesis*.** Calling to memory past matters. More specifically, citing a past author from memory.

***anaphora*.** Repetition of the same word or group of words at the beginning of successive clauses, sentences, or lines.

appeal to evidence. A line of argumentation based on accepted fact.

***arête*.** Fulfillment of purpose or function, especially the act of living up to one's full potential; moral excellence.

boasting. Talking about oneself in a self-admiring way.

cellular organization. A movement or organization composed of small, loosely connected groups that provide a flexible, adaptable model for growth based on community, local knowledge, and discipleship.

***chiasmus*.** Repetition of ideas or grammatical structures in inverted order.

chiastic parallelism. See *chiasmus*.

***conduplicatio*.** A general term for repetition sometimes carrying the more specific meaning of repetition of words in adjacent phrases or clauses.

core. A small group of dedicated leaders who serve as the foundation of a movement or an organization.

cumulative case. A case based on multiple logical supports that can survive without any one given support.

discipleship. The act of mentoring followers, based largely on the development of personal relationships; transforming someone from being the recipient of a message to being an active participant in that message.

energia**.** A genuine and appropriate show of emotion.

enthymeme. An abbreviated and more powerful form of a syllogism in which a premise or conclusion is merely implied.

epiplexis**.** A rhetorical device in which the speaker reproaches the audience in order to incite or convince them.

epizeuxis**.** Repetition of words with no others between, for vehemence or emphasis (e.g., "Verily, verily").

ethos. The persuasive appeal of one's character, and especially how this character is established by means of the speech or discourse; one of the three modes of persuasion.

eunoia**.** The feeling of friendship and goodwill that is evoked by the rhetor. As defined by Aristotle, *eunoia* is an element of both pathos and ethos.

false dilemma. A situation in which two alternative points of view are held to be the only options when in reality there exists one or more other options that have not been considered.

figures of parallelism. Using the same pattern of words to show that two or more ideas have the same level of importance.

figures of repetition. Uses of the repetition of words, phrases, or structures to generate pathos.

heuristics. A "rule of thumb" that while not universally applicable can be a pragmatic tool for evaluating the right course of action in a given situation.

imagery. The formation of mental images, figures, or likenesses of things or of such images collectively.

logos. As defined by Aristotle, an argument from reason; one of the three modes of persuasion.

mesodiplosis**.** Repetition of the same word or words in the middle of successive sentences.

metaphor. A rhetorical trope that describes a first subject as being similar or equal to a second subject in some way.

narrative. A narrated account; a story.

outreach. The process by which individuals in an organization or movement attempt to gain new followers or converts, reaching out to those opposed to or unaware of the organization or message.

parable. An extended metaphor told as an anecdote to illustrate or teach a moral lesson.

parallelism. A balance of two or more similar words, phrases, or clauses.

pathos. The appeal to emotion; one of the three modes of persuasion.

phronesis. As defined by Aristotle, the virtue of moral thought; usually translated "practical wisdom," sometimes as "prudence."

ploce. The repetition of a single word for rhetorical emphasis.

polysyllogism. Sometimes called multi-premise syllogism; a string of any number of syllogisms such that the conclusion of one is a premise for the next. See also *sorites.*

reductio ad absurdum. Latin for "reduction to the absurd." A type of logical argument where one assumes a claim for the sake of argument, derives an absurd or ridiculous outcome, and then concludes that the original assumption must have been wrong as it led to an absurd result.

rhetor. A person who engages in rhetoric; an orator.

rhetoric. The art or technique of persuasion through the use of oral, visual, or written language.

self-reporting. Listing qualifications that are necessary to establish your credibility with your audience.

shared artifacts. Past events, stories, or pieces of communication (e.g., the Bible, the works of Shakespeare, the life of Jesus Christ) with which the majority of an audience is familiar.

shared values. Values that many people hold in common.

simile. A comparison of two unlike things, typically marked by the use of "like," "as," "than," or "resembles."

small group. One of the cells in an organization; also a limited collection of individuals that shares a common goal or set of beliefs and reinforces itself through mutual respect, trust, and discipleship.

sorites. A series or chain of connected enthymemes; sometimes seen as, and certainly can be, a logical fallacy since the rapidity of claims and reasons does not allow the unstated assumptions behind each claim to be examined.

supporting material. All of the materials, media, and tools used to sustain a message and communicate it to adherents of the message.

syllogism. A kind of logical argument in which one proposition (the conclusion) is inferred from two others (the premises); consists of three parts—the major premise, the minor premise, and the conclusion.

syllogismus. The use of a remark or an image that calls upon the audience to draw an obvious conclusion. Like a rhetorical enthymeme but more compact and frequently relying on an image.

tactical flaw: Revealing a weakness that wins sympathy or shows the sacrifice you have made for the audience.

train-the-trainer. The process by which disciples are not merely trained to follow but to lead, replicating the discipleship model with other cells in an organization.

tricolon. Three parallel elements of the same length occurring together in a series (e.g., Julius Caesar's "Veni, vidi, vici").

SCRIPTURE INDEX

GENERAL INDEX